Thanks for the privilege and opportunity to visit
the great battle sites
country. With best wis
Christmas.
Fran an

FOR KING

THE NEWFOUNDLANDERS IN THE GREAT WAR

The Western Front, 1916-1918

A Social History and Battlefield Tour

by N. M. Christie

FOR KING & EMPIRE; VOLUME X

CEF BOOKS
2003

National Library of Canada Cataloguing in Publication
Christie, N.M.
The Newfoundlanders in the Great War: the Western Front, 1916-1918/ by N.M. Christie
(For King & Empire: v. 10)
ISBN 1-896979-23-8
1. Great Britain. Army. Royal Newfoundland Regiment–History. 2. World War, 1914-1918–Campaigns–Western Front. 3. World War, 1914-1918–Regimental histories–Newfoundland and Labrador. 4. World War, 1914-1918–Battlefields–France—Guidebooks. 5. World War, 1914-1918–Battlefields–Belgium—Guidebooks. I. Title. II. Series: Christie, N.M. For King & Empire; 10.

D547.N55C47 2003 940.4'12718 C2003-902106-8

Published by: CEF BOOKS
P.O. Box 40083
Ottawa, Ontario,
Canada, K1V 0W8
613-823-7000; cefbooks@rogers.com
http://members.rogers.com/cefbooks/CEFHP.html

Other books in this series

Volume I:	*The Canadians at Ypres, 22nd-26th April 1915*
Volume II:	*The Canadians on the Somme, September-November 1916*
Volume III:	*The Canadians at Vimy, April 1917*
Volume IV:	*The Canadians at Passchendaele, October-November 1917*
Volume V:	*The Canadians at Arras, August-September 1918*
Volume VI:	*The Canadians at Cambrai, September-October 1918*
Volume VII:	*The Canadians at Amiens, August 1918*

Future Volumes

Volume IX:	*Other Canadian Battlefields Of The Great War, 1915-1917*
Volume XI:	*Sacred Places; Canadian Cemeteries of The Great War, 1914-1918*

Front cover: The Newfoundland Memorial Caribou, Beaumont-Hamel. (N.Christie)

Acknowledgements: The Author would like to thank Sheila Hanratty and Hugh Nangle of Ottawa, Dave and Linda Horton of Manotick, Ontario, Daisy Rheaume of Brockville, Joanne Neville (CWGC, Ottawa) and Jan Verdoot, Poperinge, Belgium.

Beaumont-Hamel

Is it the sigh of the night-wind in the grasses,
The long rank grasses that grow so tall and thin?
Or only the cry of a night-bird as it passes
On wings of fear this field incarnadine?

Is it the soft low rustle of the garments
Of those high souls who nobly laid their all
On this grim altar of unnumbered torments,
And won to Life through deaths heroical?

Is it the sob of Earth in deadly sorrow
At the red flood that chokes her hidden ways, -
Sick with her longing for the fruitful furrow,
Faint with the memory of bygone days?

Is it the voice of God within us, calling, -
Deep unto deep - the God without, within, -
Bidding us loose our souls from their enthralling,
Moulding His Peace through this sore discipline?

John Oxenham
(1852-1941)

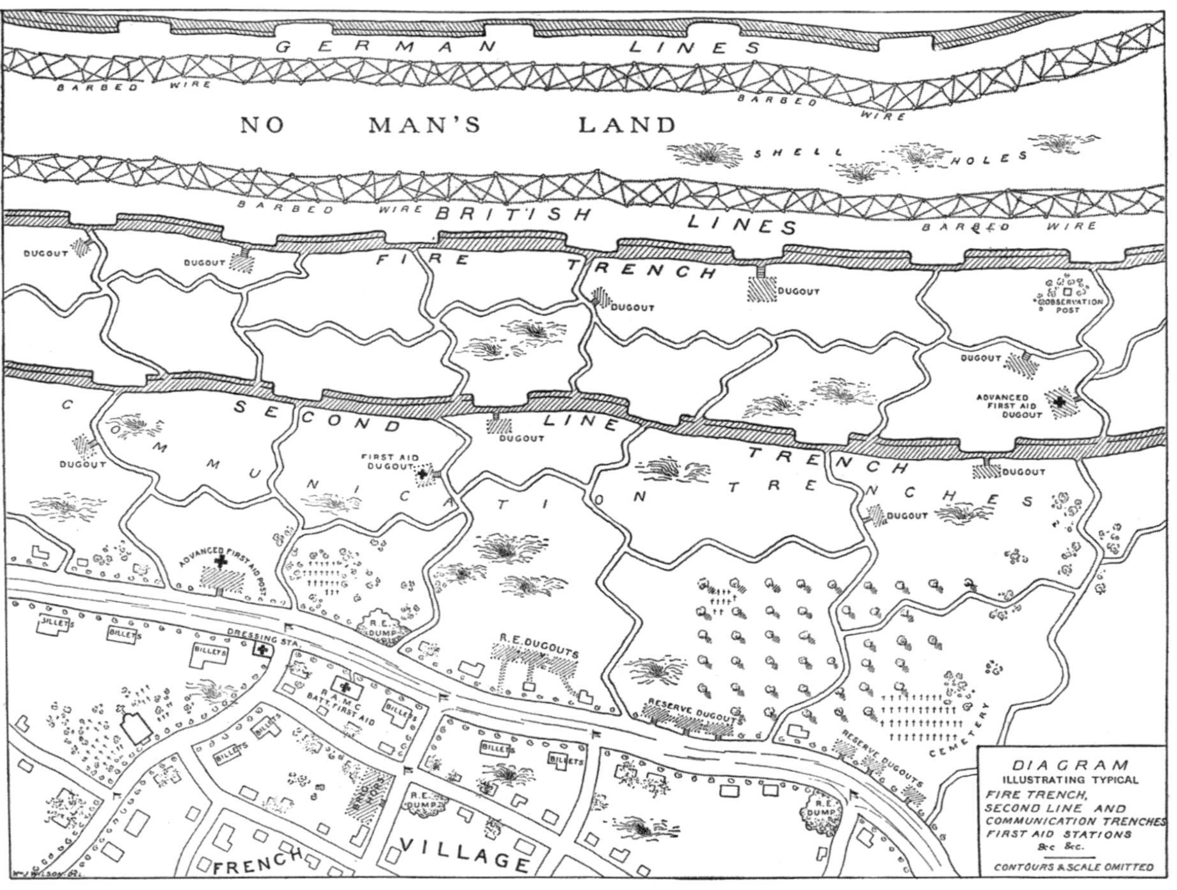

Trench systems 1916.

Table of Contents

The grave of Private Alfred E. Cake, the Newfoundland Regiment, in Vis-en-Artois British Cemetery. Cake was killed in action April 14th, 1917. He was 16 years old. (N. Christie)

Introduction

The story of the First World War was one of tragedy and sacrifice and in no corner of the world was the sacrifice greater than in Newfoundland. Like all other parts of the British Empire, Britain's oldest Colony, Newfoundland, rejoiced with the coming of war in 1914. Men across the Island responded to the Call of Mother England and in throngs they enlisted. Their reasons for joining up varied, but whether it was patriotism, unemployment, or revenge, no one was going to miss the "Great Adventure."

For Newfoundland war was very much a family affair. Mostly native-born this band of brothers and cousins proudly left all behind in support of King and Empire. In an atmosphere of great euphoria the young men of Newfoundland marched off to war.

Over the next four years the Newfoundland Regiment fought in some of the most historic battles ever fought by the British Empire. They were the only non-British participants in the first day of the Battle of the Somme, July 1st, 1916, the most infamous day in British military history. On that day the British Army suffered 60,000 casualties. Of the 801 men of the Newfoundland Regiment who went over the top that morning, 710 were lost, including 264 killed, in a matter of minutes.

In the Battle of Arras in April, 1917 the British and Canadians broke through the German lines on a 20 km front. The Newfoundland Regiment was to follow up the great victory. On April 14th, 1917 at Monchy-le-Preux the Newfoundlanders attacked into the jaws of German resistance. Despite their great courage, and against desperate odds the Newfoundland Regiment failed to advance. In a few hours they lost 460 men.

In November 1917 once again the Newfoundlanders were part of the Battle of Cambrai. In a brilliant stroke of genius the British launched a surprise attack using massed tanks. This was the first time in history that such an attack had been mounted and it met with great success. They smashed the impregnable Hindenburg Line. Finally it appeared the breakthrough was at hand. But again the Germans were not ready to give up. On December 1st, 1917 they launched a major counter-stroke that surprised the British, won back most of the lost territory, and inflicted heavy casualties. It was a devastating and demoralizing defeat.

Newfoundland lost more than 400 men.

These were not the only battles in which the Newfoundland Regiment fought. They were at Gallipoli in 1915, fought twice at Passchendaele in 1917, and were in the Battle of the Lys in 1918. Most were brutal battles and the Newfoundlanders always seemed to be in the vanguard of an attack or in the wrong place, at the wrong time. Even by First World War standards they were truly soldiers of misfortune.

Their losses between 1914-1918 are staggering. Of the 4,212 Newfoundlanders who fought on the Western Front, 1,300 died. The men who died came from all parts of Newfoundland and their deaths left a deep scar on the small communities that dot the Island. Nowhere was there a deeper cost of war.

Today the legacy of the Newfoundland Regiment is remembered through the majestic bronze caribou memorials that mark their five most significant battlefields. It is known as "The Trail of the Caribou". In small parks at Gueudecourt, Monchy, Masnieres and Courtrai Basil Gotto's unique masterpiece marks the exploits of the Regiment.

But at Beaumont Hamel, the Gotto's Caribou overlooks the most amazing First World War park. This preserved battlefield is a memorial to the Newfoundlanders who fell there on July 1st, 1916, but it is far more than that. Beaumont Hamel gives us the sense of what battle meant in 1914-1918. No where else can someone comprehend what it meant to go "Over the Top", and glimpse into another time. The park at Beaumont Hamel is the most important memorial on the Western Front.

This book serves as a guide to the five First World War battlefields commemorated by Newfoundland, and is a tribute to the Boys from St John's, Come-By-Chance, Grand Falls and other places who gave their lives in the Great War and rest in the soil of France and Belgium.

The Trail of the Caribou

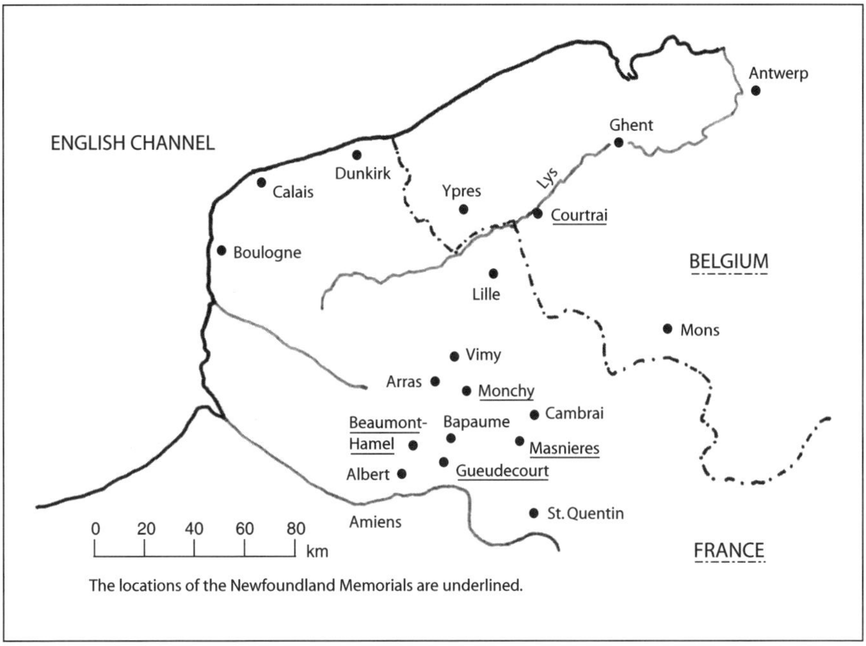

The locations of the Newfoundland Memorials are underlined.

The locations of the five Memorial Caribou.

1) Beaumont-Hamel, Somme. Commemorates the sacrifice of the Newfoundland Regiment on July 1st, 1916. It is located in the most impressive memorial park on the Western Front.

2) Gueudecourt, Somme. Commemorates the role and sacrifice of the Newfoundland Regiment in the Battle of the Transloy Ridges, October 12th, 1916.

3) Monchy-le-Preux, east of Arras. Commemorates the actions of the Newfoundlanders in the Battle of Arras (First Battle of The Scarpe), April 14th, 1917.

4) Masnieres, south-west of Cambrai. Commemorates the actions of the Newfoundland Regiment in the Battle of Cambrai, November 20th to December 7th, 1917.

5) Courtrai (or Kortrijk), Belgium. Commemorates the fighting of the Royal Newfoundland Regiment in the Final Advance in Flanders, September-October, 1918.

Getting There

This guide recommends Arras as the centre of operations for visiting the Newfoundland battlefields. Arras is located in the Pas-de-Calais and is easily accessible from Paris (170 km) and Brussels (120 km). From London, it is a two-hour drive to Dover, a 75 minute ferry ride to Calais, and a 45 minute drive from Calais. The opening of the Channel Tunnel has made a direct rail link from London to Lille, France, which is 45 minutes from Arras. Rental cars are available in any of the above-mentioned cities and tourist offices can supply routes and details of hotels.

In Arras very little English is spoken so brush up on your French before you leave. Most stores close between noon and 2 p.m., always be sure to get all your film and other necessities before lunch!

The Euro has replaced the French (and Belgian) Franc. The current exchange rate for Euros is roughly 1.50 Canadian dollar per Euro (2003). Always visit the Tourism Office to obtain information on accommodation and events of interest.

Theft is a real problem in France -particularly car break-ins. The local thieves will drill the lock, take what they want and be gone in seconds. Do not leave anything in plain view in your car and try to leave your vehicle within sight if possible. You have been warned.

What To Bring

Weather is very changeable in this part of Europe. For example, the average temperature in Belgium in July varies from 12° to 24°C. Days can start sunny and change quickly to rain, hail or even a sprinkling of snow. Above all, be prepared for wet weather.

Other than the obvious, a passport, traveller's checks and appropriate clothing, bring the following to ensure a successful trip:

-a bottle opener and cork screw
-binoculars
-a camera (with 400 ASA film)
-a compass
-rubber boots
-Michelin maps No.51, 52 and 53 (preferably the Commonwealth War Graves Commission overprint, showing all the cemeteries, available at the CWGC Office at Beaurains)
-a journal to record the details of your visit (because you will forget)

About Arras

To be consistent with other guides in this series Arras has been recommended as your centre of operations for visiting the Newfoundland Battlefield Memorials. However there is excellent accommodation in Amiens and Cambrai. To visit the Somme the small town of Albert is a good place to stay and close to Beaumont-Hamel Park, Avril Williams' Guest House at Auchonvillers is a true marvel.

Arras is the capital of the Artois region of northern France. Historically it has been the scene of many wars and the objective of many invading armies. This was the case during the First World War when the Germans briefly overran the city in 1914, and were driven out after a brief occupation. Arras was never far from the frontline and throughout the next four years was constantly bombarded. Its beautiful architecture was badly damaged by the shell-fire and it gained the reputation of being a "martyred " place, much like Ypres. Virtually every soldier who fought in the war knew Arras. It is in many ways, one of those soulful cities that was deeply engraved on the consciousness of the Great War generation.

It is the perfect place to visit the First World War battlefields. The Somme is only 25 km south, Cambrai is 30 km east and even Ypres is only 100 km north.

Arras has been witness to much warfare over the centuries. Of Roman origin, it was a stronghold in Julius Caesar's day. It was originally called Atrebatum after a tribe which lived in the area, the Atrebates. Arras is a corruption of that name.

Arras became part of the kingdom in France in the mid-17th century, prior to that it successively belonged to the Counts of Flanders (850-1180), to the Counts of Artois (1180-1384), to the Dukes of Burgundy (1384-1492) and finally to the Kings of Spain (1492-1640).

Birth place of Augustin Robespierre, Arras was not spared during the Revolution. In 1793, Joseph Le Bon, sent there on a mission, organized the Terror. The guillotine was permanently erected in the Place de la Comédie. Travellers avoided Arras and the local merchants stopped doing business.

During the Great War, the Germans occupied Arras for only three days, September 6th-9th, 1914. But after their departure, the

"Martyrdom of Arras" began. Bombardment began October 6th, 1914. Gunners fired ceaselessly on the military quarters and the two famous squares. The Hôtel de Ville, the Abbey of Saint Vaast and the Cathedral were burned down. By April 1917, Arras was completely in ruins. In March 1918, when the great German Offensive began, the bombardments broke out anew. Inhabitants were evacuated but by the end of August, the British had driven the enemy out for good.

During the Second World War Arras was captured by the Germans in May 1940. Just south of Arras British Armour gained a brief victory over Nazi General Erwin Rommel's marauding Panzers. There is a Royal Tank Corps Memorial opposite the Town Hall in Beaurains. Arras was finally liberated in September 1944. Behind the Citadel is an impressive Memorial to those shot by the Germans. The Mur Des Fusliees is a spooky reminder of Nazi atrocities and is well worth a visit.

A visit to Arras should begin in the architecturally-unique Grand'Place, once an orchard belonging to the Abbey of Saint Vaast, and the Petite-Place. For hundreds of years these squares have been bordered with gabled private houses and edged with stone columns and elliptical arches supporting vaulted galleries.

Merchants once drew crowds of buyers to their stalls under the porticos of the squares and the famous tapestries of Arras were once made in the damp cellars under the galleries.

Bordering the west side of the Petite-Place is the Hôtel de Ville, above which rises the graceful silhouette of the belfry. Long the centre of town, the Petite-Place attracted the townspeople to public meetings, festivals and public executions.

Today, the tourist office is located at the Hôtel de Ville (03 21 51 26 95) and is open daily. From there, guided tours can be arranged of the underground tunnels beneath the town hall (35 minutes, year-round). First used as cellars, the tunnels often served as shelters for the population during invasions and for the soldiers of the First World War. You can also visit the belfry.

Arras is famous for its "cobalt blue" porcelain, first produced in the late 18th century. It is available in most tourist shops in the town centre.

Accommodation is not a problem in Arras. You may want to check out the following hotels:

Astoria, 10 place Foch, 62000 Arras, tel. 03 21 71 08 14

Hôtel Ibis, place Viviani, 62000 Arras, tel. 03 21 23 61 61

Hôtel Moderne, 1 boulevard Faidherbe, 62000 Arras,
tel.03 21 23 39 57
Ostel des 3 Luppars, 47 Grand'Place, 62000 Arras,
tel. 03 21 07 41 41

Some Other Possibilities

Avril Williams' Guest House, 10 Rue Delattre, Auchonvillers, 80560, Somme, tel. 03 22 76 23 66.
Hotel de La Basilique, 5 rue Gambetta, Albert, 80300, Somme, tel.03 22 75 04 71.
Hotel de la Paix, 41 rue Victor Hugo, Albert, 80300, Somme, tel. 03 22 75 01 64.
Novatel, CD 934, Longeau, 80440, Boves, tel. 03 22 46 22 22.
Ibis, 4, rue du La Mal de Lattre de Tassigny, 80000, Amiens.
La Ferme du Bois Gallant, CD 929, Querrieu, Somme, tel. 03 22 40 13 42.

Bed and Breakfast in the Somme Area

Sylvie and Mike Byott, Flers, Somme, tel. 03 22 85 13 71.
Mme Pecourt, Mailly Maillet, Somme, tel. 03 22 76 28 79.
Julie Renshaw, Auchonvillers, Somme, tel. 03 22 76 28 79.
Mme Belangez, Grandcourt, Somme, tel. 03 22 74 81 58.

The Make-up of an Army

The Army - The British Expeditionary Force on the Western Front was divided into four or five Armies. Throughout the war the entire B.E.F. varied in strength, but usually employed 4,000,000 (1917) soldiers in the field. An Army was made up of between two and four Army Corps. During the Battle of the Somme the Newfoundland Regiment belonged to the Fourth British Army.

The Army Corps - An Army Corps consisted of a number of Infantry Divisions, depending on its needs. The Corps was commanded by a Lieutenant-General. Its numeric strength varied, but it could put as many as a 120,000 men in the field. In July 1916 the Newfoundland Regiment belonged to VIII Army Corps.

The Division - An Infantry Division was composed of three Infantry Brigades, associated Engineers, Artillery, Medical, and Supply staff, etc. At full strength it contained 20,000 soldiers of which 12,000 were infantry, 3,500 artillerymen, 2,000 Engineers or Pioneers and 750 men in the Medical Section. It was commanded by a Major-General. From 1915 to early 1918 the Newfoundland Regiment was part of the 29th (Imperial) Division.

The Brigade - An Infantry Brigade was composed of four Infantry Battalions (reduced to three Battalions in 1918). Each Brigade had its own engineers, signals, field ambulance, trench mortars and machine gun unit. It was commanded by a Brigadier-General. From 1915 until early 1918 the Newfoundland Regiment belonged to the 88th Infantry Brigade.

The Battalion - The Infantry Battalion consisted of 1,000 men. This was the theoretical strength of the unit, but after Headquarters staff, illness, leave, wounded, etc. were deducted, a Battalion could normally put 600-700 rifles in the line. It was commanded by a Lieutenant-Colonel. Each Battalion was made-up of four Companies (200 men), commanded by a Major or Captain. In turn, the Company was broken down into four Platoons, each commanded by a Lieutenant, and each Platoon was divided into four Sections, each commanded by a Sergeant.

The Newfoundland Regiment, 1915-1918

The 29th Division

86th Brigade	87th Brigade	88th Brigade
2nd Battalion Royal Fusiliers	2nd Battalion South Wales Borderers	4th Battalion Worcestershire Regiment
1st Battalion Lancashire Fusiliers	1st Battalion King's Own Scottish Borderers	1st Battalion Essex Regiment
1st Battalion Royal Dublin Fusiliers	1st Battalion Royal Inniskilling Fusiliers	2nd Battalion Hampshire Regiment
16th Battalion Middlesex Regiment	1st Battalion Border Regiment	1st Battalion Newfoundland Regiment

In December 1917 the title of the Newfoundland Regiment became The Royal Newfoundland Regiment.

After the fighting in the spring of 1918 the Newfoundland Battalion was so under strength that it was removed from the 29th Division and used as G.H.Q. (General Headquarters) Troops. In September 1918 the Regiment was once again transferred to a fighting Division. They joined the 9th (Scottish) Division, 28th Infantry Brigade during the Advance to Victory. They were brigaded with the 2nd Battalion, Royal Scots Fusiliers and the 9th Battalion, Scottish Rifles. Due to manpower shortages British Brigades had been reduced to three infantry battalions by September 1918.

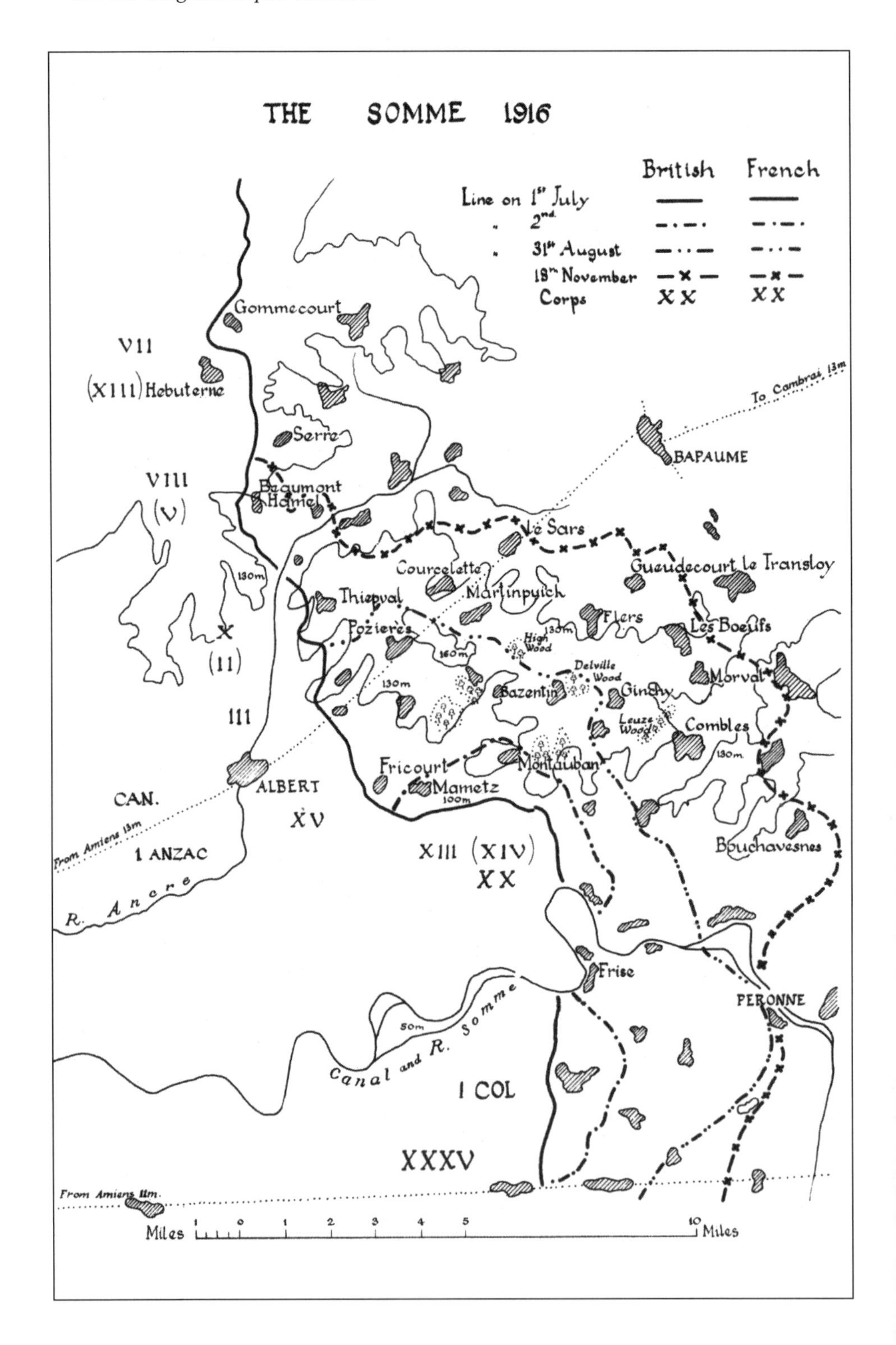
THE SOMME 1916
British
French
Line on 1st July
2nd
31st August
18th November
Corps
XX
XX
Gommecourt
VII
(XIII) Hebuterne
Serre
VIII
(V)
Beaumont Hamel
X
(II)
III
CAN.
1 ANZAC
XV
ALBERT
From Amiens 13m
R. Ancre
To Cambrai 13m
BAPAUME
Le Sars
Courcelette
Gueudecourt
le Transloy
Thiepval
Martinpuich
Pozieres
Flers
Les Boeufs
High Wood
130m
160m
130m
Delville Wood
Bazentin
Ginchy
Morval
Leuze Wood
Combles
130m
Fricourt
Montauban
Mametz
100m
XIII (XIV)
XX
Bouchavesnes
Frise
PERONNE
50m
Canal and R. Somme
I COL
XXXV
From Amiens 11m
Miles
10
Miles

Historical Overview
The Battle of the Somme
July-November 1916

Newfoundland at War

With a population of only 242,000 Newfoundland was Britain's smallest lion in August 1914. But when war was declared, like all others across the British Empire, the call of the Mother Country could not be refused. Immediately the Government of Newfoundland offered a force of 500 men. Their offer was accepted and more than 500 enthusiastic volunteers quickly enlisted. In October 1914, amidst cheering crowds, 537 men of the First Newfoundland Contingent, clad in navy blue puttees, marched through St, John's, to a Hero's send-off. Few could have anticipated what the future held.

At sea they joined the convoy carrying the 30,000 men of the First Canadian Contingent and by October 20th, 1914 the "Blue Puttees" were encamped with the much larger Canadian Contingent on the Salisbury Plain.

Proud of their heritage, which was distinctly not Canadian, the Newfoundlanders wished to remain a separate entity and not be absorbed into the Canadian or British armies. They formed their own Battalion of The Newfoundland Regiment and waited for more men to arrive to bring them up to full battalion strength. In December 1914 they were transferred to Scotland and over the next few months received an additional 1,000 reinforcements. The nature of the Island itself ensured that many of those who enlisted knew each other, and many were brothers and cousins. Going to war for Newfoundland was very much a family affair.

In August 1915 orders were received that the 1st Battalion, The Newfoundland Regiment, was to proceed to the Mediterranean. The men were issued tropical kit and embarked for Egypt. There they were to join the regular British Army formation, the 29th Division in Gallipoli. This Division was made up of some of the most famous Regiments in the British Army. It was no small honour and perhaps a bit intimidating for the Newfoundlanders to be in such fine company.

The Regiment arrived at Suvla Bay, Gallipoli on September 20th,

1915. They were fortunate to escape the bloody battles against the Turks on the peninsula, battles that had raged since April; but Gallipoli was still a deadly place. Over the next few months their lives were relatively safe. The campaign was winding down and before long the decision to evacuate was made, and the Newfoundlanders' biggest task came in assisting the evacuations at Suvla Bay and Cape Helles.

By January 9th, 1916 this little episode of the Battalion's history had ended with only 38 dead. After a brief respite in Cairo the 29th Division was ordered to France. They arrived on the Somme in April 1916. Over the next two months the Newfoundlanders rotated in and out of the front lines. They suffered their first casualties on the Western Front. However this was small change, for in a short time they would be part of the largest British Offensive thus far in the war. It was to be known as The Battle of the Somme.

The Germans on the Somme

The Somme region of France is beautiful, undulating farmland. The region takes its name from the Somme River, a pretty, meandering stream that is known for its fishing and wildlife. The region is checkered with small farming villages and in 1916, these villages such as Beaumont-Hamel, Thiepval, Mametz, Fricourt and Pozieres gained infamous reputations.

As the Somme battlefield lacks any particularly advantageous physical characteristics, the Germans had built a complex of interconnecting trenches and deep redoubts across the rolling chalk hills. They took full advantage of every contour. To protect themselves from observation, the Germans generally entrenched on the down side of a slope. The trenches were deep and solid, often strategically interconnected with other trenches, known as Switch Trenches. A warren of communication and support trenches was utilized for transporting supplies, reinforcements and ammunition. The redoubt positions were often connected by tunnels coming from a variety of places in the support lines. In front of the trenches were dense belts of barbed wire. Farms and villages had been fortified and linked by a maze of underground works. Each position was designed to extract a great price from any attacker.

The Battle of The Somme - The British Plan

In the autumn of 1915 and the winter of 1916 the British Army had been rapidly building up its force opposite the German lines on the Somme (also known as Picardy). Since the outbreak of war the area had been a quiet sector, and during the lull the Germans had fortified all the best positions in a countryside of undulating ridges, small woods and villages.

The idea was to attack these positions utilizing massive numbers of soldiers and artillery on a 28 km front. The plan for the Battle of the Somme was quite straight forward. They would use thousands of guns of all calibres and bombard the German trenches with a ferocity previously unseen in warfare. For seven days they would pulverize the German positions. The shelling would cut the barbed-wire entanglements, collapse the dug-outs and kill the occupants. Then the soldiers, heavily-laden with 30 kilograms of equipment, would climb out of their trenches, walk to the German lines and capture the few survivors.

In a similar manner, the next line of infantry, following a creeping barrage, would continue on and take the next line of trenches and then break through into the open countryside. At this point cavalry would carry on and make the victory complete. It was simple British ingenuity. The fact that a similar plan, tried in 1915, had failed, did not deter the Generals.

Many of the British soldiers to be used in the first phase of the Somme fighting were Kitchener's men. Like the Newfoundlanders these were the enthusiastic volunteers that had flocked to join the Colours in 1914. They had enlisted in groups from the same factory or community or even church group. They were known as the "Pals". Some of these 100,000 men of the Pals Battalions had seen some action, but for many the Somme would be their first real taste of battle.

The Plan for the 29th Division

The role of the 29th Division on July 1st, 1916 was to advance behind the British barrage, break through the German positions, and advance for 4 km. At Zero Hour, 7:30 am, the infantry of the 86th and 87th Brigades (8 Battalions comprising 8,000 men), would be responsible for capturing the front line German trenches in front of the village of Beaumont-Hamel. After one hour, at 8:30 am, the supporting infantry of the 29th Division, the four Battalions of the 88th Brigade, including the Newfoundland Regiment, would follow through the first wave of attackers, and continue the assault to the German second line.

Preparations for the Attack of July 1st

"June 30th was a beautiful day, very little work was done and everyone was in the best of spirits. In the afternoon a draft of 66 new men arrived and the majority of those took part in the attack next day... Here were a thousand or so Newfoundlanders - fishermen, lumbermen, trappers and men from the city just spending their last few free minutes together before falling in; falling in for the last time until the curtain had rung down on the tragedy of Beaumont-Hamel... At 9 pm The Regiment fell in. When the roll was being called another regiment that was to attack on the morrow marched past. By ten minutes past nine all company commanders had reported their companies correct, the CO mounted his horse and rode to the head of the column, then with a wave of his hand commenced the last march to Beaumont-Hamel...

"... When darkness had fallen the Battalion fell in ready to march. The noise of guns seemed very near now, the sky appeared to be illuminated with incessant sheet-lightening... The weary, aggravating tramp up the long communication trench came to an end and by 2 am on July 1st, the Regiment was settled away in St. John's Road and Clommel Avenue from which trenches the attack was to be delivered. These trenches were comparatively new, having been dug by the Regiment and were in rear of the line that we usually held when in the forward sector. St. John's Road was so christened by the 2nd South Wales Borderers as a compliment to the Regiment. The SWB put the finishing touches to the trench after the Newfoundlanders had broken the back of the work.

"For officers there was no rest but the men, very tired after five hours marching, were soon asleep except of course for sentries, etc., Lewis gunners overhauled their guns and each man was roused in turn to have his equipment inspected. Another tedious duty was the issuing of further battle stores to those previously detailed to carry them. These stores consisted chiefly of trench bridges and ladders, to be carried by two men each, and bangalore torpedoes... With inspections and issue of stores having been completed, there was only the wait for zero hour... Most of the men dozed, the officers strolled about their various commands chatting to groups in each fire bay and giving final little bits of advice, cigarette smoking was allowed and altogether it was very much like the final few minutes before a big football match.

"The British artillery was keeping up a continuous roar; so much firing was going on that the sharp crack of the field guns was almost reduced to nothing by the ceaseless rush of the shells overhead. Slowly the sky in the East grew lighter and as day broke a last meal was taken by all ranks... At 6 am everybody was alert and the final wait had commenced."

Captain Arthur Raley, MC, CdeG, Adjutant, Newfoundland Regiment

The attackers would be assisted by artillery and the exploding of a large mine under the main German redoubt on Hawthorn Ridge.

The German defences in front of Beaumont-Hamel were particularly strong. They had dug in and heavily wired their trenches and the hollow that ran behind the lines held many German troops. In addition a deep ravine, called Y Ravine was just behind the front. Y Ravine was thick with dugouts and provided a natural defensive feature. It could not be observed by the British. To compound matters the ridges east of Beaumont-Hamel gave German artillery a commanding view of the British trenches. All movement could be observed.

The Bombardment Begins

On June 24th, 1916 along a 28 km front the British guns opened fire. Over the next seven days more than 1.5 million shells would hit the German positions. The enemy lines disappeared under a shower of steel and fire. On the night of June 30th-July 1st, 1916 the infantry, 150,000 in the first wave, moved into their jump-off positions and waited for Zero Hour. Each Division, each Battalion knew their job. In a few hours they would be on their way to Berlin!

The men of the Newfoundland Regiment were not scheduled to be in the first wave of the assault. They moved into positions on the night of June 30th and were held in reserve in a Communication Trench known as St. John's Road, south of the village of Auchonvillers and a few hundred metres from the British front line. There they waited their orders. The 801 men from Newfoundland hugged the walls of the trenches as the massive barrage flew overhead. The noise of the bombardment was deafening as these men huddled with their friends, brothers and cousins, anticipating their turn at battle. They were safe for the moment.

At 7:20 a.m., through the din of explosions, the men felt a massive rumble, followed by the ignition of tons of ammonal. It was the Hawthorn Ridge mine going up under the enemy position in front of Beaumont-Hamel. Now they waited the final ten minutes for the attack to begin.

The Battle Opens

At 7:30 a.m., Saturday, July 1st, 1916, the barrage subsided and the British troops climbed out of their trenches. They made their way towards specifically cut gaps in their barbed wire and started the descent across No Man's Land towards the German line. The men anticipated minimum resistance, but instead they were met by a wall of machine-gun and artillery fire. The attackers stumbled and fell. Bravely they tried to push on, but in the face of such resistance there could be no advance. The initial assault towards Beaumont-Hamel had met a stunning defeat.

The centre piece of the Generals' plan had failed. The artillery had not destroyed the German dugouts and killed the occupants. Much of the enemy's barbed wire was still uncut, and to make matters worse, the Germans had much more artillery that had been anticipated. The attacking soldiers, now dead or stranded in No Man's Land, had no idea what had hit them.

Opposite the 87th Brigade the Huns had come out of their well-protected dugouts in "Y" Ravine, placed their machine-guns on the parapet of the trench and mowed down the attackers. The firing was so intense the German machine-guns over-heated. The enormous British barrage had eliminated any hope of surprise and the enemy knew the attack was coming.

By 8 a.m. the British lines were in complete confusion. The shock of their overwhelming rebuff, along with difficulties in communicating what was happening in the battle, gave conflicting information to the Generals. They must not have believed their attack could be stopped so completely. In addition, they received erroneous messages indicating that some men were into the German lines. The decision was made to support those men by ordering a further attack. A second wave tried to advance, but was met with withering fire and was also repulsed. Less than 30 minutes into the assault, the attack of the 87th Brigade was over and No Man's Land was strewn with more than 2,000 of their dead and wounded.

A lull came over the battlefield and finally at 8:45 a.m. orders were given to renew the assault. In spite of the morning's failures the Newfoundlanders were instructed to follow the original plan.

Newfoundlanders to the Attack!

At 8:45 a.m., the 1st Battalion, The Newfoundland Regiment, was ordered to attack. The men were crowded in the support trenches 250 metres behind the main British line. They were not aware of what had happened to the first waves. As they moved out they found the commu-

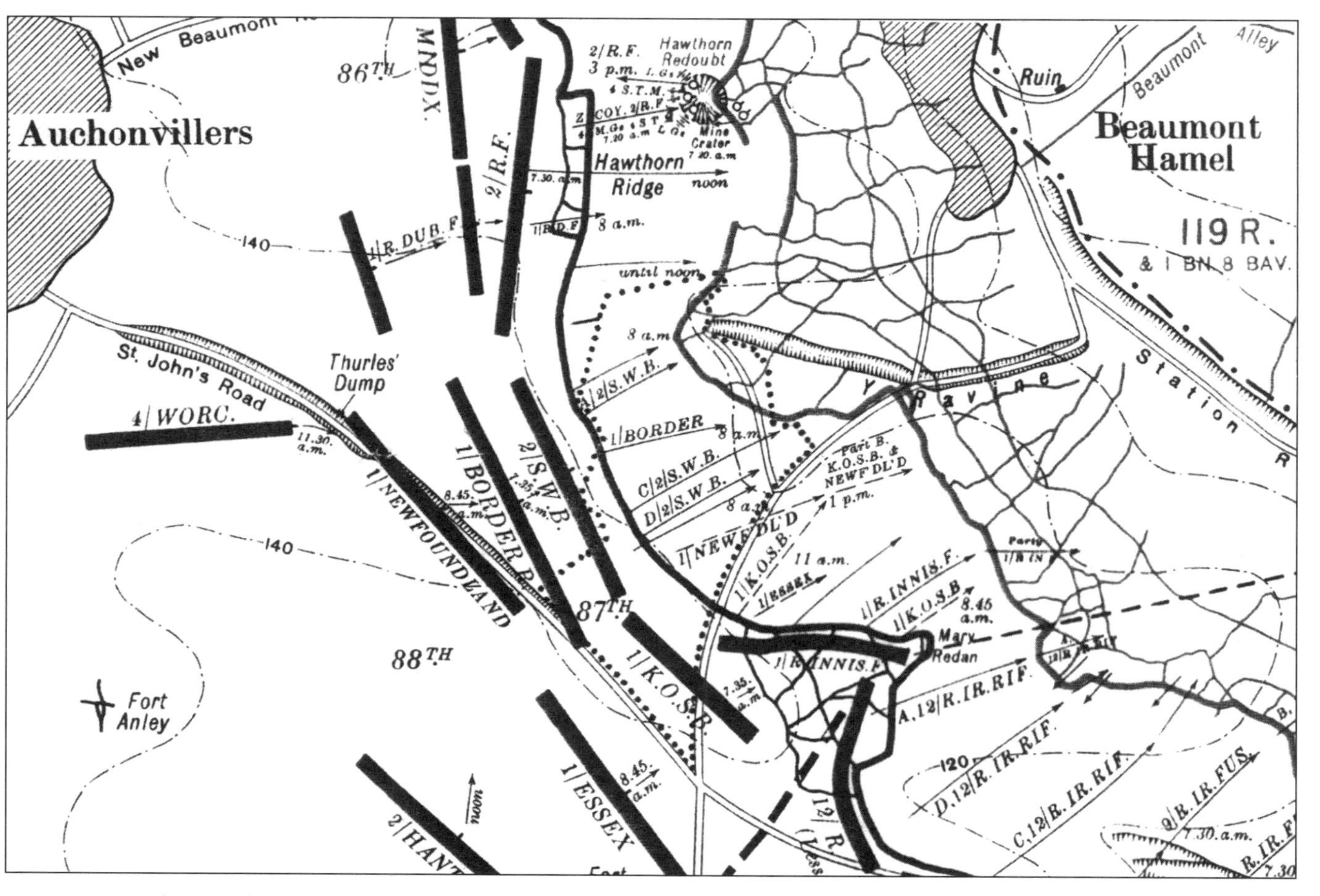

The Attack at Beaumont-Hamel, July 1st, 1916 (Park boundary is marked ....)

nication trenches blocked with wounded, and had great difficulty getting forward. Due to the congestion they realized they could not reach the front lines in time to comply with the order to attack by using the trenches. The decision was made to advance overland. This meant they would have to cross 250 metres of open land before even reaching No Man's Land.

Loyal to the end, the Newfoundlanders climbed out of their trenches and moved up the gradual rise towards the main British trench-line. They could not even see the German trenches they were to attack.

By the time the advance commenced it was 9:15 a.m. and the battlefield was strangely quiet. The only visible movement was the silhouettes of more than 700 Newfoundlanders negotiating around the shell holes and through the barbed wire. The German observers on the overlooking ridges probably could not have believed their eyes. They focussed their artillery and machine-guns on the small band of approaching men. The fury of the fire must have come like a curtain of death. Soldiers were bowled over by the raining shrapnel explosions; men collapsed as the machine-gun bullets tore through them. Some covered their faces as if walking in a hail storm. The wounded crawled into shell holes for protection. The Newfoundlanders were being annihilated.

Before they had even made the British front line trench, many had fallen. As the survivors made their way to a gap cut in the British wire, their advance slowed and the Germans targeted this congested group of men. A small party collected near a clump of trees just outside the wire tried to gain their bearings and then proceeded to continue down the slope towards the enemy. Their remaining officers urged them on, but the attack was suicide. The German machine-gunners had the attackers silhouetted on the horizon and continued to exact a terrible toll. Before long the attackers were all gone. They had vanished in a torrent of steel. In under half an hour the pitiful advance had been snuffed out. The battlefield was littered with the dead and wounded of Newfoundland and their comrades of the 29th Division. The battle was over.

It was rumoured that a few Newfoundlanders made it into the German wire and a handful made it into the enemy trench But this is unlikely. The attack had been an awful mistake.

Back at headquarters there were once again plans to renew the attack, but that order was thankfully cancelled. The Generals now realized the magnitude of their defeat and the vulnerability of their own positions. Immediately all available men were ordered forward to establish a defensive line to thwart any German counter-attack. Fortunately the enemy did not come.

Saturday, July 1st was a beautiful summer's day. A clear blue sky belied the horrors of battle. Over the next hours there was a frantic effort to remove the casualties. The following day the Germans allowed an informal truce and many of the seriously wounded were evacuated from No Man's Land and hundreds of corpses received quick burial on the battlefield. The surviving Newfoundlanders had to bury many of their friends. The shock of July 1st left many in a dazed state. They could not have comprehended what had just happened.

The final tally was horrible. The Newfoundland Regiment, the only non-British battalion that attacked on July 1st, lost, in less than 45 minutes, 266 dead and 446 wounded. They were not even in the main attack; they did not even enter the German trenches! Little Newfoundland, Britain's oldest colony, was devastated by that single day of terrible carnage. Of the 801 Newfoundlanders in the attack, eighty-nine percent were casualties.

Throughout small communities across Newfoundland, telegrams to unsuspecting families were delivered. It was the same everywhere, whether it was St. John's, Moreton's Harbour, Fogo Bay, Trinity Bay, Channel or Bay Roberts. No family was untouched by the futile slaughter at Beaumont-Hamel.

In St. John's the Ayres received the shocking news that four members of their family were killed on July 1st. Captain Eric Ayre and two of his cousins, Gerald and Wilfred, died with the Newfoundlanders; his only brother, Bernard, was killed the same day serving with the Norfolk Regiment.

Privates Fred and George Abbott, sons of Henry and Emily Abbott of St. John's, were both killed July 1st. Privates J. Roy and Stewart Ferguson, sons of Daniel and Isabella Ferguson of St. John's, also fell at Beaumont-Hamel. The closeness of the communities emphasized the tragedy.

Sadly the failure of the Newfoundlanders on July 1st was not unique. The British attacks in the north, at Gommecourt and Serre, had all been repulsed with heavy losses. The 29th Division lost 5,000 men

The Attack, July 1st, 1916

"At 7:15 am the hurricane bombardment opened. The noise was now kept at a steady pitch; there was no break in the sound at all; in fact it seemed as if the sound was felt rather than heard, the air seeming suddenly to increase in weight.

"Again an officer was sent to synchronize watches, this time in the front line trenches that were held by the South Wales Borderers. Watches were synchronized between 7:15 and 7:20. At 7:20 am above the bombardment, was felt the concussion and trembling of the earth as the ground in front of Beaumont-Hamel shot like a fountain into the air and at the same moment the SWB ran up the trench steps and out into the open. The artillery fire lulled for a second or two and then along the whole battle front it lifted and became a "barrage".

"From the very start it was obvious that the enemy were not only extremely well prepared for an attack but were actually expecting it. Before the Newfoundland officer had finished synchronizing his watch wounded men of the SWB were flopping back over the parapet. In spite of our tremendous gun fire the enemy machine gunners and riflemen were firing as only well-trained troops could.

"... Though no news came through to the Newfoundlanders there was a general feeling things were not quite as they should be. The enormous volume of machine gun fire from the enemy lines and the short time it seemed to last, at first made one hopeful that all was well and that they were being put out of action by our troops. This hope was dashed with each fresh burst of fire as the British made their repeated attempts to advance... at 8:20 am orders were received to stand-by and wait for further orders... 8:40 came and went... At 8:45 the telephone rang and the verbal order was received from Brigade...At 9:15 am Brigade was notified... "The Newfoundlanders are moving".

"The Battalion was to advance from St. John's Road and Clommel Avenue, that is to say, from the rear line of trenches, and this necessitated passing through narrow gaps in four belts of wire, all of which were on the side of a slight hill running down towards the enemy. A more deadly piece of ground to cross, in the formation the Battalion had to adopt to pass through the wire, it is hard to imagine.

"Steadily they advanced to the first line of wire under a heavy machine gun, first from the right and then from the whole front. Men began to drop, but not in great numbers, as the enemy had his guns trained on the gaps. The first gaps were reached and men fell in each of them, those who could not go on did their best to clear the gaps of wounded, killed and equipment.

"Try to imagine the attack at this stage. The Newfoundlanders just start-

ing the advance, no other troops were advancing on left or right of them, every machine gun in the area firing at high pressure at pre-arranged targets and the first line of wire is passed by A and B Companys with heavy casualties and attack is only two minutes old... They were now struggling through the second belt and pushing onto the third belt. Men were falling faster now, the machine gun fire was appallingly heavy but the steadiness of the men was quite unshaken. On they went with never so much of a waver anywhere. Each man as he fell, if life were still in him, endeavoured to roll out of the way of his comrades, there to lie until those wonderful Newfoundland stretcher-bearers found them. The only visible sign that the men knew they were under this terrific fire was that they instinctively tucked their chins into an advanced shoulder as they had so often done when fighting their way home in a blizzard in some little outport in far off Newfoundland.

"By this time the enemy artillery had commenced a barrage along our front wire and were also bombarding, though not heavily, the area over which the troops were advancing... It seemed impossible that men could live to get through those gaps, yet here and there a man would be seen to dash forward as if bursting through a hedge. Here and there could be seen an officer, looking for men to lead. They were through the last belt now, but oh! How few... Just the same steady walk continued. In one case, towards the left of the line, a section advanced on the last belt almost intact - or possibly others had joined it. In the rear of the this section walked two men carrying a ten-foot trench bridge. As the section approached the gap men began to fall in ones and twos until, at the gap all were down except the two men with the bridge. At the entrance to the gap the leading man of the two was hit and, as he fell, brought down the bridge and his partner. Without the least sign of flurry, the second man got up, hoisted the bridge onto his head and slowly picked his way through the now crowded gap. Whether the German machine gunners withheld their fire in admiration is not known but this hero stolidly advanced until he could advance no further... All this advance lasted 20 minutes...

"The trenches were literally packed with wounded and dead of all Regiments. The heat was unbearable and added to this was the incessant bursting of heavy shells on parapet, traverse and in the trench. Wounded men who had managed to crawl a little rolled down into the trench, falling with a sickening thud on the bottom or some wounded comrade and there they lay under a sweltering sun, groaning and waiting for a stretcher-bearer

"No words of mine can give a fair account of the advance. It was just a steady walk forward of several hundred Newfoundlanders, each one knowing that he was going to be hit, but determined to carry out his orders until he could advance no further."

Captain Arthur Raley, MC, CdeG,, Adjutant, Newfoundland Regiment.

out of the 8,000 that participated in the attack opposite Beaumont-Hamel. At Serre 10,000 were killed, wounded or missing.

The total statistics demonstrate the scope of the tragedy. Along the entire length of the battle front, on July 1st alone, the British Army suffered 57,540 casualties, including 20,000 dead. The shock of this failure rocked the British public. Many of the soldiers killed came from the same towns, lived on the same streets, worked together and belonged to the same clubs and churches. As a result, the losses of that one day of battle profoundly affected the British people.

In mid July the Newfoundland Regiment was withdrawn from the Somme, reinforced and sent to Ypres. But they had not seen the last of the Somme fighting.

Postscript - The Battle of the Ancre, November 13th, 1916

After July 1st, 1916 the Somme battle was waged opposite Fricourt, south of the Ancre river, the scene of that day's only successful attack. The northern battlefields, disastrous failures on July 1st at Serre and Beaumont-Hamel, were largely forgotten until the end of the Battle of the Somme. In an attempt to force the Germans back from the heights overlooking the small river the British command decided on a major assault north of the Ancre, from Serre to Hamel. The attack would involve five divisions and would follow a similar strategy as employed on July 1st. The dubious honour of attacking over the ground so bloodied with the men of Newfoundland fell to the 51st Highland Division.

The 51st Highland Division had already distinguished itself on the Somme. Its infantry were all kilted, and its battalions represented the most famous Scottish Regiments: the Gordons, Seaforths, Argyll & Sutherland Highlanders and The Black Watch. Ominously the attack would be preceded by the blowing of a second Hawthorn Ridge mine, in the exact location as on July 1st. To the north and south of Beaumont-Hamel, a new batch of troops were going to try their luck against the impregnable German positions.

At 5:45 a.m. on Monday, November 13th, 1916, the second Hawthorn Ridge mine went up signalling the start of the attack. In the morning light the Highlanders advanced quickly and took the German front lines. But the enemy fought back from Y Ravine, and their machine-guns inflicted heavy casualties on the Scots. Gradually they

Sergeant Stewart S. Ferguson
St. John's. Age 26.
Killed in action July 1st, 1916.
Commemorated on the Beaumont-Hamel Memorial.
His brother J. Roy Ferguson was killed the same day.

Private George B. Hatfield
St. John's. Age 22.
Killed in action July 1st, 1916.
Commemorated on the Beaumont-Hamel Memorial.

Company Sergeant Major Victor W. Miles
Age 31.
Killed in action July 1st, 1916.
Commemorated on the Beaumont-Hamel Memorial.

Private James J. Howard
Bonavista Bay. Age 22.
Killed in action July 1st, 1916.
Commemorated on the Beaumont-Hamel Memorial.

forced their way around the Ravine, with the task of clearing it of Germans falling to the 14th Battalion of the Gordon Highlanders. In vicious hand-to-hand fighting using grenades and bayonets they accomplished the job.

To the north other Highland units were in the village of Beaumont-Hamel, and to the south the 63rd Royal Naval Division had captured Beaucourt. The fighting was ferocious and a constant rain from countless exploding shells killed many men. By late afternoon it was clear they had achieved a costly, but courageous victory. Further north opposite Serre, the German positions were once again too much for the attackers and the attack had failed.

Evidence of the Highlanders' successful attack is found in Newfoundland Memorial Park. Two Memorials were placed there by the 51st Division and their fallen share the cemeteries, and often the same grave, with the men of the 29th Division killed on July 1st.

The Battle of the Somme ended officially on November 18th, 1916. It had cost the British Army almost 500,000 casualties, including 250,000 dead. It was truly the death of a generation.

Bombarding German Trenches, Beaumont-Hamel, 1916. (PANF)

Private Martin J. Cahill
Conception Bay. Age 25.
Killed in action July 1st, 1916.
Buried London Cemetery & Extension. VI. C.26.

Captain Michael F. Summers
St. John's. Age 26.
Died of wounds received July 1st, July 16th, 1916.

Private Harold Hutchings
Bonavista. Age 19.
Killed in action July 1st, 1916.
Buried Ancre British Cemetery, VI.F.11.

Private William Fowler
(true name William Clarke)
Brigus.
Killed in action July 1st, 1916.
Buried Ancre British Cemetery, Special Memorial 33.

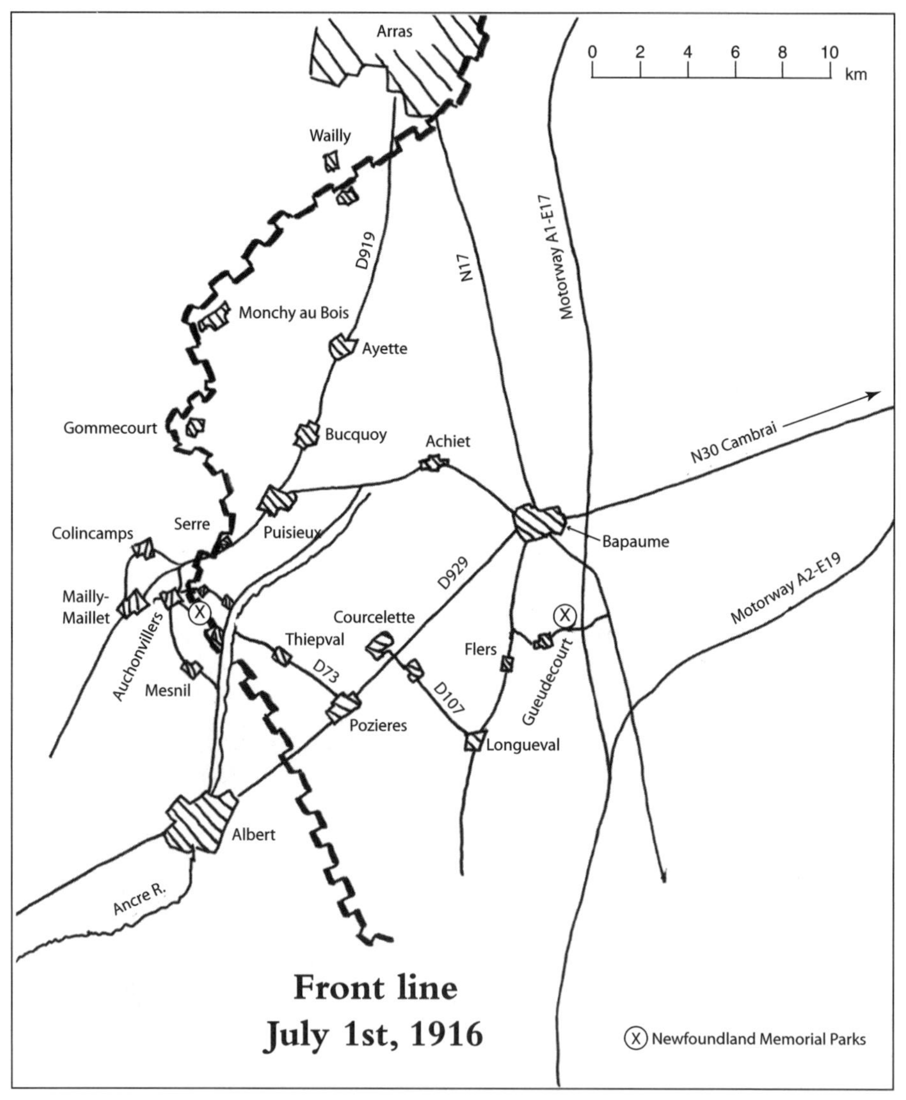

Route from Arras to Beaumont-Hamel.

The Tour - Beaumont-Hamel, July 1st, 1916

Leave Arras by following the road (N17) leading south to Bapaume. After 2.5 km turn left on the D60 at Beaurains (it will also be marked by the sign to the Commonwealth War Graves office). A further 1.5 km the D60 meets with the D919 towards Amiens. Follow the D919 through Ayette, Bucquoy, Puisieux, and Serre. Continue past the large British and French cemeteries at Serre, and after 1.8 km turn left on the D174 to Auchonvillers. This turn is well-marked with a Canadian sign for Beaumont-Hamel Battlefield Park. Follow the D174 into the village and take the D73 to Hamel. The Park is 1.3 km south-east of the village on the D73. After 1 km you will notice a British Cemetery on your left in the farmer's field and beyond it a clump of trees. (The cemetery is Hawthorn Ridge No.1 and the trees are growing out of the 1916 Hawthorn Ridge mine crater.) When you reach the parking lot opposite the Park, stop.

NOTE: The area over which you have just travelled was fought over several times during the First World War. During the Battle of the Somme the area from Arras to Serre was behind German lines. The Allies regained the territory when the enemy withdrew to their Hindenburg positions in February, 1917. The Germans recaptured it in March 1918 and it was retaken by British troops in August 1918, in the Final Advance to Victory. There are many cemeteries marking this fighting and if time prevails, they are worth a visit. Amongst the many burials at Bucquoy Road are British soldiers killed when France fell in May, 1940. The Indian-Chinese cemetery at Ayette is very interesting, as are the two large British Cemeteries at Serre.

The 2 km between Serre and the Auchovillers turn-off was the scene of heavy fighting on July 1st, 1916. Like the attack at Beaumont-Hamel, it was a costly repulse for the attacking British soldiers, costing 10,000 men killed and wounded.

Beaumont-Hamel Newfoundland Memorial Park is staffed by Canadian Guides, April to November, to give tours of the Park. There is also an excellent Visitor's Centre, which gives an impressive interpretation of the battle.

Move to the northern end of the parking lot.

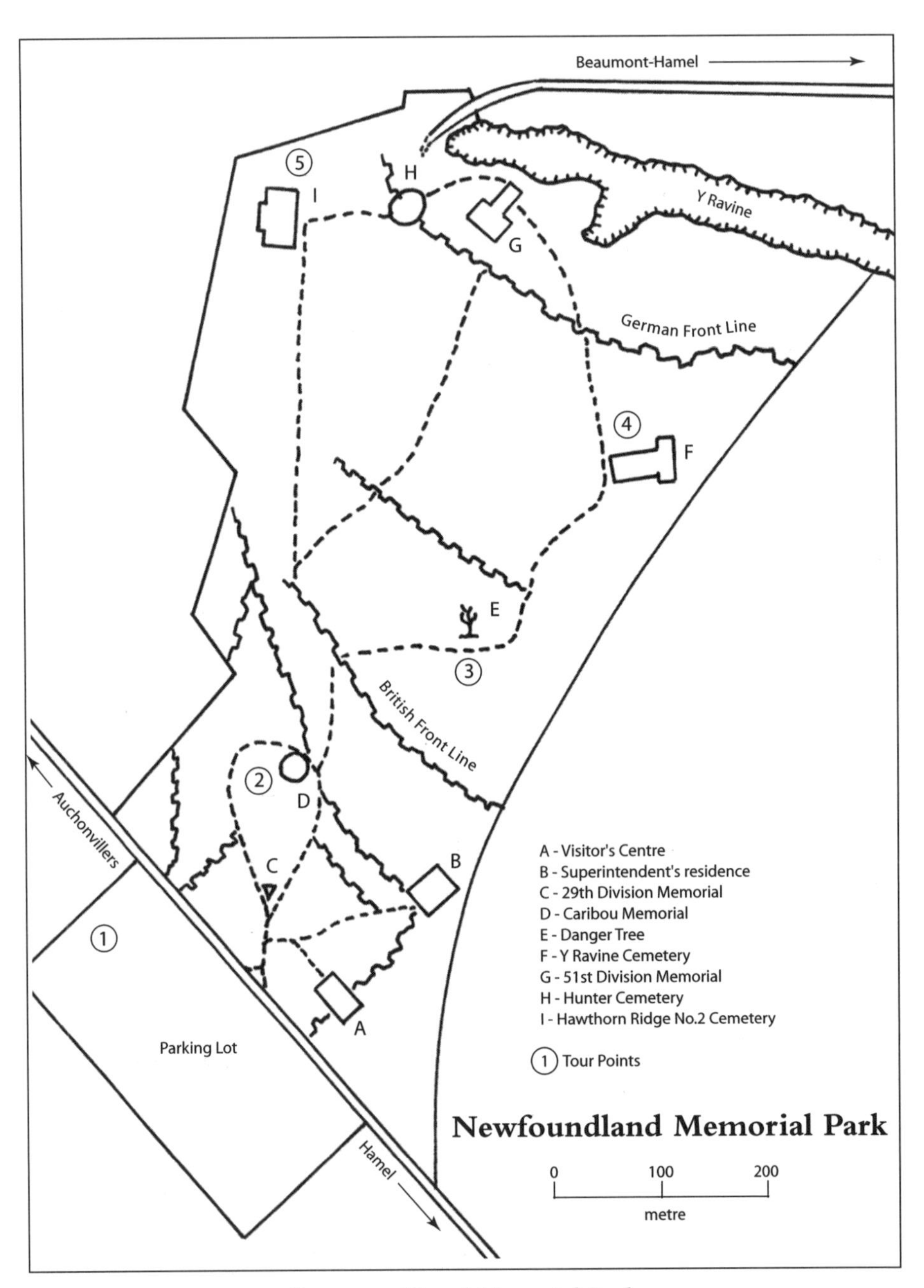

Beaumont-Hamel Memorial Park.

Point 1; St John's Road; Orientation to the Battlefield

One of the challenges in understanding the Somme battle is to envisage what this beautiful rolling countryside looked like in 1916. The Battlefield Park is now surrounded by trees and is deceptive in that the trees limit the overview. The trenches of 1916 ran continuously along the ridges in front of you and Communication Trenches snaked out a path connecting the villages and back areas with the front line. Looking south across the farmer's field a British cemetery (Knightsbridge) is nestled in a hollow 600 metres away. One of the many Communication Trenches (CT) that connected the rear areas with the front ran by this cemetery. Looking north to Auchonvillers another main CT ran south of the village. These CT were vital links to the front on the night of June 30th/July 1st, 1916. It was through the CT south of Auchonvillers that the Newfoundland Regiment moved up into their positions. In the meantime the other attacking battalions advanced by Knightsbridge and likewise men got in position all along the 28 km stretch of the great offensive.

The Newfoundlanders, being in support of the first wave, settled into a trench known as St. John's Road, that ran along the D73 just in front of you. Here, crowded in the trench they waited through the massive barrage.

Looking south, the British trenches ran just east of the D73, down into the Ancre river valley, 1.7 km away. The lines then climbed up onto the Thiepval ridge and then continued south well beyond view. Keep oriented by locating the massive Thiepval Memorial to The Missing. It is sometimes obscured by the trees.

Just for reference the village of Beaumont-Hamel is located 1.4 km north-east of you, but is in a hollow. The only notice you will get of it is the view of the church steeple from time to time.

The Newfoundlanders were in St.John's Road when the Hawthorn Ridge mine went up at 7:20 a.m., and waited there through the din of machine-guns and artillery fire indicating the attack of the first wave. Surely their anxiety, fear and excitement must have been powerful as they waited their turn. After 30 minutes there was a surprising lull in the firing. The minutes passed before they received the word to advance. They had no way of knowing what befell the first wave. They had no idea of what they were being asked to do. The 800 men of the Newfoundland Regiment prepared to move out.

Although blocked by the trees of the Park the Hawthorn Ridge crater, now full of trees, is 1.2 km north of you (and 100 metres north of Hawthorn Ridge Cemetery, No.1).

To follow the route taken by the Newfoundland Regiment walk through the entrance to the Park, past the Newfoundland Government plaque (it's worth reading the poem by John Oxenham near the entrance). When you reach the 29th Division Memorial (the Red Triangle mounted on a stone cairn) turn left into the maze of old trenches.

It was in this area the Newfoundlanders found the CTs leading to the front congested with wounded. (The morning attacks had suffered 2,000 casualties.) It was here that the decision was made to leave the trenches and advance to the front overland. One by one they climbed over the parapets. As their numbers grew the Germans, observing the lines, called for artillery; and shrapnel was soon raining over the advancing soldiers. They were still 200 metres from the Jump-off positions. Their organization, initially an orderly advance was quickly thrown into disarray.

You can well imagine the view of 801 Newfoundlanders rising up from the trenches, each man trudging onwards carrying 30 kg of equipment. Here the first of many fell under the weight of German steel.

Make your way through the old trenches to the Caribou Memorial and climb to the top.

Point 2: The Caribou Memorial

From the top of the Memorial you can get a clear view of the battlefield. There is no other place where you can get such a clear understanding of a First World War battle. The British front runs north-south, the complex of trenches, although they have subsided over the years, are still evident. Gone are the belts of barbed wire which would be thick between the British trenches as well as in front of the main line facing No Man's Land. This barbed wire was to cost the Newfoundlanders dearly.

The orientation arrows on the monument help in distinguishing the battle. From the Memorial, 500 metres away, are the German front lines, marked forever by the 51st Highland Memorial in the centre and Y Ravine Cemetery off to your right. The plan called for the

The Danger Tree, 1922. (R. Cochius)

The field of fire, looking towards the German lines (marked by the 51st Division Memorial indicated by the arrow). (N. Christie)

51st (Highland) Division Memorial. (N. Christie)

Plaque at the entrance of the Park. (N. Christie)

29th Division Memorial. (N. Christie)

Newfoundland Regiment to cross this ground, without effective artillery support, and capture the German front line.

Looking back from the Caribou you can imagine how many would have fallen trying to negotiate around the trenches and shell holes and through belts of wire. This slowed the attack and gave the German gunners more time to focus on the only attacking force in their field of fire.

Move to the front of the monument.

The attack had been going for less than 15 minutes when the men passed the base of the monument. Some hid their faces from the torrent of shrapnel and bullets that ripped their ranks. That had only 30 metres to go before they could launch their attack. By this time they had probably lost more than 200 men.

Just off to your right the survivors reached the front line wire but found it uncut. They had no way to get through, except through pre-cut gaps made by the British prior to the attack. The gap in the wire was off to your right and it was through this narrow gap that the men funnelled through. Once again they had to slow down and became even easier targets for the Germans. There the enemy intensified and the Newfoundlanders fell in droves.

Climb down from the Memorial and follow the path to the right, through the British front line, until you get to the Danger Tree.

Point 3: The Danger Tree

The Danger Tree is the location where the gap in the barbed wire came out into No Man's Land and it was here the men, confused and disorganized, tried to unite and move on to their objective. By now the remaining soldiers, urged on by one of the few surviving officers, Lieutenant Hubert Herder, started their attack. In the previous 15 minutes the German shrapnel had inflicted a terrible toll, but now, singled-out in No Man's Land, silhouetted against the sky, they were perfect targets for machine-gunners firing from across the entire front. line. Never in the whole assault did the Newfoundlanders waver. In the face of certain death they came on. The attack continued on until none remained. Later, there was a rumour that a few made it into the German barbed wire, and even one man, Private Thomas Carroll got into the enemy trench, but this is unlikely.

From the Danger Tree, look down into the hollow where Y Ravine Cemetery is located. This was the direction of the Newfoundlanders'

Y Ravine Cemetery and the Danger Tree from the British front line. (N. Christie)

British front line running north from the Caribou Memorial. (N. Christie)

attack.

Walk down to Y Ravine Cemetery.

The Thiepval Memorial and the Ulster Memorial can be seen through the trees on your right. As you walk along you are passing over the ground where the last Newfoundlanders gave their lives. By the time you reach the cemetery you will have reached a point further than any man of the Newfoundland Regiment advanced on the sunny Saturday morning of July 1st, 1916.

Point 4: Y Ravine Cemetery

From Y Ravine Cemetery look back towards the Danger Tree and the Caribou Memorial. This is the German view of the attack. It is easy to imagine a German machine-gunner locating his targets as the men struggled through the gap in the barbed wire and it is easy to see why the Newfoundlanders had no chance against these positions. Looking over to the 51st Highland Memorial you can follow the German front line, but what you do not see are the tunnels and deep dugouts where the Germans sheltered and easily withstood the British bombardment.

From the German positions it is clear how they preferred to locate their trenches on the downside of a slope, where they could not be easily observed. Other positions located on ridges behind the frontline gave them not only a great field of fire, but the advantage of clear observation.

Y Ravine Cemetery is one of three Commonwealth War Graves Cemeteries in the Park. It contains the graves of 428 Commonwealth soldiers, including 45 Newfoundlanders. Many of the graves belong to men of the 29th Division killed on July 1st, 1916.

Among the Newfoundlanders buried here is Lieutenant H.C. Herder, who so valiantly led his men in the attack from the Danger Tree.

Walk along the path towards the 51st Highland Division Memorial.

The 51st Division finally captured these positions on November 13th, 1916, four and a half months later. Their attack was better planned than that of July 1st. They had a short bombardment of only 45 minutes which gave them the element of surprise. They also dug an advance Jump-off trench only 200 metres from the German lines so that their men had a shorter distance to reach the German line. It is still visible today.

After the war the veterans of the 51st Division chose Beaumont-Hamel as the place to commemorate their achievements and sacrifices. They had fought twice in the Battle of the Somme; in the Battle of Arras; Third Ypres, the first major tank battle at Cambrai, thrice during the great German offensives in 1918 and played a significant role in the Advance to Victory. The impressive statue was modelled on Company Sergeant Major Robert Bowen of the Highland Light Infantry.

From the Monument, looking back to the Newfoundland Caribou, you can get a clear understanding of the impressive German field of fire on July 1st, 1916.

Walk around the monument to the wooden cross at the head of Y Ravine.

The cross is another memorial to the 51st Division. Originally it was erected in High Wood to mark the brutal action there on July 14th, 1916. It was relocated to Beaumont-Hamel after the war.

From this location you get an understanding why Y Ravine was so important and made the German position so strong. The dugouts that lined the sides of the ravine were dug so deep into the chalk subsoil that they were virtually shell-proof. They were also spacious chambers and could easily hold a front line garrison. Unfortunately for the attackers on July 1st, most of the German positions on the Somme were constructed in such a fashion. In the mid 1990s soil blocking a ventilation shaft leading into a Y Ravine dugout subsided, and for the first time in decades the dugout could be accessed. The chambers were quite large and 50 feet deep and connected to the head of Y Ravine. It was hoped at one point they could be opened to the public, but to date nothing has transpired. The covered shaft can be seen in the tall grass behind Hunter's Cemetery.

From the top of Y Ravine Beaumont-Hamel is only 600 metres down the dirt track. The village was also captured on November 13th, 1916 by the 51st Division.

Continue on the path to Hunter's Cemetery.

Hunter's Cemetery is the second of three Commonwealth War Graves Cemeteries in the Park. It was made immediately after the fighting on November 13th, 1916 when the dead of the battle were collected and buried in a large shell hole. After the war the mass grave was landscaped into this unique design. It contains 46 soldiers of the 51st Division.

Continue on to Hawthorn Ridge Cemetery, No.2.

Point 5: Hawthorn Ridge Cemetery, No.2.

While walking towards the cemetery you can see the Memorial Cross from Hawthorn Ridge Cemetery, No.1 just north of the Park and the trees growing out of the hole created by the blowing of the Hawthorn Ridge mines of July 1st and November 13th. The British front lines ran along from the Caribou to the two Hawthorn Ridge cemeteries and over the ridge towards Serre.

From the cemetery you get a different angle on the Newfoundland attack of July 1st, this time from the perspective of other British soldiers who watched the tragic advance. This area had also been the scene of carnage that morning when the 1st Border Regiment, 2nd Royal Fusiliers and the 2nd South Wales Borderers of the 29th Division were shot down in the first and second waves of attack.

This is the third Commonwealth War Graves Cemetery in the Park. It was made in the spring of 1917 when the remains of those killed on July 1st were buried here. The bodies had laid out on the battlefield for 8 months and very little of the corpses was left. It contains 153 graves, although 65 are unidentified. Amongst the 24 Newfoundland graves is Private Thomas Carroll who was thought to be the only Newfoundlander to get into the German trenches on July 1st (based on where his body was found it is unlikely he got near the German lines).

Return via the front of the Caribou past the Newfoundland Memorial to the Missing to the Parking lot. The next leg in the tour is by car and goes into the Ancre River valley and then up to the memorials on Thiepval ridge. You will be driving through the historic heartland of the Somme Battlefield. There are a number of exceptional memorials and impressive cemeteries along the route that should be visited.

Turn south onto the D73 towards Hamel. You are driving along the July 1st, 1916 British front line. A brigade of the 36th (Ulster) Division attacked here on July 1st with no success. On November 13th, 1916 it was once again attacked, this time successfully, by the 63rd (Royal Naval) Division. The road descends down into the Ancre river valley and into the village of Hamel. In the village turn left on the D50 and after 300 metres turn right on the D73, crossing the railroad track and a small bridge. (Ancre British Cemetery,

View north from atop the Thiepval Memorial. The Ulster Tower (right arrow) and Beaumont-Hamel Park (left arrow) are marked.
(N. Christie)

which contains 2,540 Commonwealth graves, including 32 Newfoundlanders, is 250 metres along the D50.) Follow the D73 up onto the heights overlooking the Ancre. After 1.1 km you will arrive at the Ulster Tower, the Memorial to the sacrifices of the 36th (Ulster) Division in the Great War.

The 36th Division was comprised of Protestant Irish soldiers. (The Catholic Irish Divisions were the 16th and the 10th. The 16th also fought on the Somme.) They suffered 5,000 casualties in this area on July 1st. Their losses were incurred from just south of Beaumont-Hamel Park to just south of Ulster Tower. The area around the Tower was a heavily fortified trench works, known as the Schwaben Redoubt. The Irish managed to get into the Redoubt, but could not be adequately reinforced, and were forced to retreat from their hard-won prize. Two cemeteries near the Tower, Connaught and Mill Road, contain many of their dead.

It is suggested to visit the Tower and climb to the observation deck at the top. From the Ulster Tower you see most of the northern July 1st, 1916 battlefield. Beaumont-Hamel Park is visible to the north-west. To the south you can see the Thiepval Memorial. This area was the scene of terrific fighting on July 1st, 1916 and again in September 1916, when these positions finally fell to British forces.

Return to your car and follow the D73 to the Thiepval Memorial, 1 km distant.

This massive monument, rising impressively (30 metres) out of the calm Somme countryside, commemorates the Missing of the Somme. Designed by Sir Edwin Lutyens and unveiled by Edward, Prince of Wales, on July 31st, 1932, the Thiepval Memorial records the names of almost 72,000 British (names are still being added) and 830 South Africans, killed in the Battle of the Somme, who have no known grave. Many of the men of the 29th Division, the men who fought side-by-side with the Newfoundlanders at Beamont-Hamel and Gueudecourt are commemorated here. From the grounds of the Memorial there is a spectacular view of Beaumont-Hamel Park in the north, Pozieres to the south and Albert to the south-west. Today it is hard to imagine that 7,000 British soldiers were killed or wounded in the fighting for Thiepval Ridge.

Exit the Memorial and return to the D73, turning right in the direction of Pozieres. After 1.1 km you pass the infamous Mouquet Farm on your left. The village 3 km ahead of you is Pozieres. In the

village and in the fields around it the Australians suffered 24,000 casualties in July-September 1916. There are two Australian monuments in the village. At the junction with D929 turn left for Bapaume (right takes you into Albert). You are driving along the Albert-Bapaume road, the scene of indescribable fighting in 1916.

On the eastern outskirts of Pozieres, 500 metres from the road junction, you pass the Tank Corps Memorial on your right and the Memorial to the 2nd Australian Division. The Tank Corps Memorial commemorates their men who fell in the Great War, 1916-1918. It states: "Near this spot the first tanks used in war went into action on 15th Sept. 1916". The Australian memorial is on the site of the Pozieres Windmill, and marks the highest point on the Albert-Bapaume road.

Three km along the D929 is the village of Courcelette. The Canadian monument is on the left of the D929, south of the village. It commemorates the sacrifice of the Canadians, in the Battle of the Somme, September-November, 1916. In Courcelette and in the fields north of it, the Canadians suffered 23,000 casualties.

To return to Arras follow the D929 to Bapaume. At Bapaume turn north on the N37 to Arras.

To visit the Newfoundland Memorial at Gueudecourt, turn right on D6 to Martinpuich and refer to the Tour instructions on Page 45.

John Oxenham's poem at the entrance to the Park. (N. Christie)

Historical Overview
The Battle of the Transloy Ridges, October 7th-20th, 1916

The Battle Rages

Throughout the summer and into the autumn of 1916, the Battle of the Somme raged. Attack after attack was delivered; each assault was always preceded by massive artillery bombardment. Small woods and fortified farms became the graves for thousands of soldiers. Usually, the onslaught would bring some territorial gains initially, but always the Germans would counter-attack and would often regain territory that had been lost. The Somme had become a battle of attrition. The price was beyond the soldier's worst nightmares, but still the assaults were ordered and the men always complied. The only argument the Generals could offer was that Germany, with a smaller population, could not replace the fallen as easily as the Allies. This logic was of little comfort to the men. The original plan of a breakthrough had been forgotten. Both armies were being bled white.

Even if an attack was successful, it did not preclude the Germans digging another trench behind another ridge. In the Battle of the Somme the Germans did exactly that. Week by week the front moved back ridge by ridge.

More often than not, the attacks on the strongly fortified German defences on the Somme proved disastrous. The artillery bombardment rarely succeeded in cutting the barbed-wire and the soldiers, trapped in No Man's Land, would be cut down in swathes by the German machine-guns. Sometimes, the Germans allowed the assault troops to enter their front-line trench. Then the German artillery would blast No Man's Land to prevent reinforcements or ammunition from reaching the newly captured position. The reinforcements would be decimated by the German barrage when crossing the open ground and the soldiers in the captured trench would be isolated. At this point, the Germans would counter-attack via communication trenches or underground subways. The German stick grenade was the weapon of choice and was a very effective killer with good range and accuracy.

The British forces continued their attempts to push northwards throughout July and August and slowly drove forward against heavy German opposition and numerous counter-attacks. Again, the loss of men and equipment was staggering. British casualties for the months of July (after the July 1st attack) and August were 160,000 men.

By the end of August, the fighting to the south of, and along the remnants of the Bapaume-Albert road had reached the outskirts of Pozieres, a small village that occupied the highest point on the road. Pozieres held a commanding view of the battlefield, and its importance did not go unnoticed by the Germans. They had fought a titanic struggle with the Australians since late July to maintain their hold on the strategic Pozieres Ridge, but had gradually been forced to give ground. The fighting was so severe in the area around Pozieres that nothing remained of the village and the battlefield was covered with the unburied corpses of Germans and Australians, intermingled, as much of the fighting had been hand-to-hand.

In September British attacks, using tanks for the very first time, gradually pushed forward the Allied line. Thiepval, an objective of July 1st, finally fell, but no German collapse was in sight. In October the 29th Division was once again ordered to the Somme. Amongst their battalions, was the now-replenished, 1st Battalion, The Newfoundland Regiment.

Since they were pulled out of the line shortly after the disaster of July 1st, 1916, The Regiment had received reinforcements, and spent August and September near Ypres in Belgium. They had suffered few casualties during that time. On October 6th, 1916 orders were received that they were to return to the Somme. This must have had an unnerving effect on the men as they entrained for the south.

The plan for the 29th Division was to participate in another Push, another attack on another German trench. This time it was against German positions on the Transloy Ridges.

The Battle of the Transloy Ridges, October 7th-20th, 1916

The Battle of Le Transloy was a continuation of the successful British Battle of Flers-Courcelette, September 15th-22nd. During this Push, British, Canadian and New Zealander forces, using tanks for the first time in history, had pushed the Germans back 2-3 km over a 10 km front, from Thiepval to Morval.

In October the weather had turned sour. Now the soldiers had to deal with the thick Somme mud in addition to the considerable and constant threat of German artillery. This was not enough to affect the Generals' enthusiasm for the offensive. By early October the British had come up against another position built on a series of ridges and spurs south of Bapaume, known as the Transloy Ridges. Due to bad weather and a need to bring up fresh troops a break in the fighting took place for a week at the beginning of October. October 7th was the date chosen to renew the assault.

The fresh troops assigned for the upcoming offensive included the 88th Brigade of the 29th Division. Their duty was to follow up the attack as required. The Newfoundlanders moved into Gueudecourt and took up positions outside the village.

At 2:05 p.m. on October 12th, 1916 men of the 1st Battalion, Newfoundland Regiment and 1st Battalion Essex Regiment attacked the German trenches, running 400 metres east of their positions. The plan was for the men to follow a creeping barrage, seize the German front line, Hilt Trench, secure it, and push on to the German second line, Grease Trench, on the crest of the ridge, 800 metres distant.

Within 30 minutes both battalions succeeded in taking Hilt Trench and shortly after captured the crest. But the Essex were driven back to their starting position, leaving the Newfoundlanders exposed. They too, were forced back to Hilt Trench. Now isolated, the survivors battled heavy artillery fire and a counter-attack by German infantry. Despite heavy losses, they courageously held on. At 9 p.m. they were relieved. Since they were engaged at Gueudecourt they had lost 239 men.

Across the British front the battle on October 12th had gained little ground, but had cost the attackers thousands of men. The weather, enemy opposition and poor preparations had lost the battle.

Gueudecourt was the final battle for the Newfoundland Regiment in the Battle of the Somme. In two actions the battalion had suffered more than 900 casualties, almost 100% of their fighting strength. They remained in the Gueudecourt-Lesboeufs area until December when they were withdrawn for a well-deserved rest.

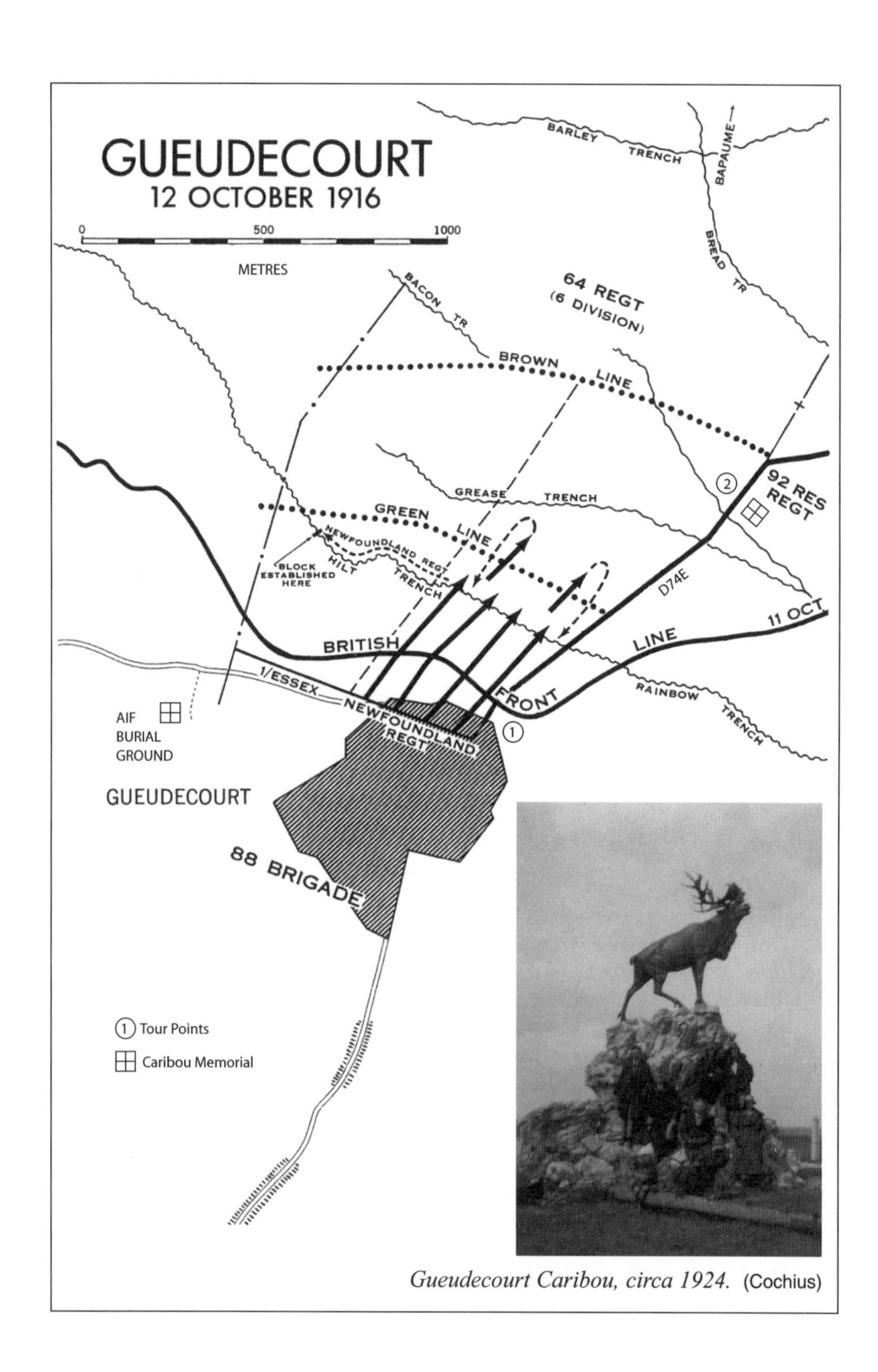

Gueudecourt Caribou, circa 1924. (Cochius)

The Tour - Gueudecourt, October 12th, 1916

Continued from the Tour of Beaumont-Hamel (Page 40).

As the D6 passes through Martinpuich, the scene of heavy fighting in September 1916, it turns into the D107. After two km you reach a large wood, Bois des Fourcaux, or as it was known in 1916, High Wood.

(NOTE: Alternative route from Arras (direct to Gueudecourt). Take N37 from Arras to Bapaume (32 km). Continue past Bapaume, still on the N17 towards Peronne. After 3.5 km you reach Beaulencourt. Take the D11 west to Gueudecourt. You will reach the Memorial after 2.2 km and the village after 3 km.)

In the days following the attack on July 1st, British forces broke the German's southern flank and on July 14th, 1916 reached High Wood. Indian cavalry crossed the fields south of you in an effort to break through, however the Germans shot down the attackers and reinforcements stopped the British advance. Over the next two months the fighting around High Wood cost many lives. As part of the Flers-Courcelette Offensive, High Wood fell to a British-New Zealander attack, September 15th, 1916. The cemetery across from the Wood, London Cemetery Extension, contains more than 3,800 graves, including 165 Second World War burials. The vast majority of the burials were remains found all along the Western Front after 1934. There are several memorials at High Wood.

Continue on to the "T" junction with the D20 left to Longueval. (On your left, one km out in the farmer's field is the New Zealand Memorial commemorating their actions here of September-October1916, during which they suffered 7,000 casualties. At the junction you will see Caterpillar Valley Cemetery and the New Zealand Memorial to the Missing directly ahead.)

At Longueval turn left on the D197 to Flers.

(A visit to the South African Memorial at Delville Wood is recommended. The South African Brigade entered Delville Wood 3,153 strong on July 14th. When they left the Wood on July 20th, less than 200 remained. There is a museum outlining the history of the South Africans in both World Wars and Korea. During the Great War 200,000 South Africans enlisted and 12,452 died.)

The three km stretch to Flers is over the ground captured on

The Newfoundland Caribou Memorial at Gueudecourt. (N. Christie)

September 15th, 1916. Continue through Flers on the D197 for 1.4 km. At the junction with the D74, turn right for Gueudecourt. (Just off the road, on your right, is the cemetery AIF Burial Ground. This cemetery is one of the "discovery of remains" cemeteries. It was used predominantly for the burial of remains found between 1924-1927.)

Continue on to Gueudecourt village, one km further on. Drive into the village, turning left on the D74E (becomes D11) to Beaulencourt. Just outside the village, stop. Look up the road to the ridge. On the ridge is a clump of trees and within the trees is the Gueudecourt Newfoundland Memorial.

Point One: Jump-off, October 12th, 1916

Gueudecourt had been entered by British soldiers on September 15th, 1916, but had not fallen until September 26th. After that, as part of a larger attack, the attacking continued, but little progress could be made up the ridges. Then the weather turned and the heavy rains turned the battlefield into a quagmire. However the Command was undaunted. They felt the morale of the Germans was down, and only a few more attacks would break their will.

Thus the attacks against these ridges continued, with the next jump-off scheduled for October 7th, 1916. Six British Divisions attacked but with little success. The Germans still held the crests and had built a substantial reserve defensive position three km behind them.

After the October 7th attack the Newfoundlanders were brought into action. On October 9th they moved up to Gueudecourt. The destruction reaped by artillery in the later stages of the Somme battle had left a scar of desolation; villages destroyed, woods splintered and burned and everywhere were the copses of friend and foe. The German shelling was of an intensity few of the men had experienced before. Gueudecourt was a ruin and a well-known target of the German gunners. In the severe shell-fire on October 10th 100 Newfoundlanders were casualties. The men spread themselves out in the trenches running north from where you are standing. It was safer in the fields than it was in the village.

The attack was to start on October 12th at 2:05 p.m.. The plan was for the Newfoundlanders to attack from their positions, capture a German trench called Hilt (mid-way from where you are standing and the Memorial on the ridge). They were to follow a creeping barrage, which would give them cover. After they reached Hilt Trench, the creeping barrage would move ahead and the Newfoundland Regiment would follow behind to capture a German position on the crest of the ridge known as Grease Trench. The German positions were not as complex as those they had met at Beaumont-Hamel, there was less wire and they were not so formidable.

For the men waiting in the wet trenches, the morning of October 12th must have passed slowly. They fixed their bayonets, had a tot of rum and waited for Zero Hour.

At 2:05 p.m. the Newfoundlanders climbed out of their positions and followed the creeping barrage. They were immediately in trouble as some men moved too close and became casualties of their own guns, as some were firing short.

View of the Gueudecourt Battlefild. The Caribou Memorial is located in the trees on the horizon. (N. Christie)

Walk along the road towards the Memorial on the ridge.

The men were not daunted, and with courage charged by a little rum they quickly reached Hilt Trench; and in close fighting, using bayonets, grenades and fists, they drove the enemy out. By 2:30 p.m. Hilt Trench had been captured.

The men pushed on to the second objective, Grease Trench. The day thus far had gone well. Their comrades, the Essex Regiment, had also succeeded in their attack. But the Germans would not yield these positions without a fight and a counter-attack was ordered.

Lieutenant Cecil B. Clift
St. John's. Age 24.
Killed in action October 12th, 1916.
Commemorated on the Beaumont-Hamel Memorial.

Lance Corporal Hardy F. Snow
St. John's. Age 21.
Killed in action October 12th, 1916.
Commemorated on the Beaumont-Hamel Memorial.

Thomas E. Rodgers
St. John's.
Killed in action October 12th, 1916.
Buried Bancourt British Cemetery, VI.F.20.

Second Lieutenant Samuel J. Ebsary
St. John's. Age 37.
Died of wounds October 15th, 1916.
Buried St. Sever Communal Cemetery.
His brother, Frederick, died of wounds in Egypt, September 23rd, 1915.

Quickly the enemy moved up by negotiating along communication trenches and attacked the Essex. The Essex were unable to hold on and were driven back, leaving the Newfoundlanders' flank exposed. They were forced to vacate the vulnerable position and retire back into Hilt Trench.

Return to your car and drive up to the Newfoundland Memorial.

Point Two: The German Counter-attacks, October 12th, 1916.

From this position you can oversee the entire battlefield of October 12th from the German's perspective. You can also see why these ridges gave the Germans such an advantage. Throughout these battles the enemy took the best positions from which they could observe any troop movements and safely hide their own men from British observation.

The distance from where you are standing to the village is 800 metres. The area in front of you was devastated in 1916; muddy shell-holes from thousands of rounds would leave the appearance of a lunar landscape. The village would be a shambles of destroyed houses. Only the British trenches winding out of the village and the German fire trench and communication trenches leading from the ridge would be visible. At 2:05 p.m. a curtain of fire enveloped the German front, and maybe through the smoke and fire the men of the Newfoundland and Essex Regiments could have be seen advancing across No Man's Land.

Within minutes the soldiers were leaping into the first position and over the next 30 minutes the sound of grenades and rifle fire would dominate. Shortly after the surviving British and Newfoundland troops would be advancing again, this time against the German positions on the ridge. Once again the creeping barrage would have offered some protection for the advancing troops.

As the Newfoundlanders reached the ridge they poured into the German trenches and for a time held the ridge you are standing on. But off to the north the Essex could not hold on, and the Newfoundlanders were dangerously exposed. German shells would rain down on them, and finally, by 4 p.m., they had to withdraw. The soldiers streamed back down the ridge to find safety in the remnants of Hilt Trench. There in the face of severe shell-fire they dug in and waited for the impending counter-attack.

They would not wait long as a force of 500 Germans was observed snaking their way forward. The Newfoundlanders used the German trench and trench blocks to fire on the attackers and stop the attack. Despite the shelling the men hung on to their hard-won gains. As darkness fell the threat of further attacks diminished and by 9 p.m. the remnants of the Newfoundland Battalion were gratefully relieved.

In their second real battle the men had performed well. They had achieved one of the few advances of the day, but at a heavy cost. Their loss was 239 men, including 120 dead. Amongst the fallen was Oswald Goodyear, who was one of three brothers from Grand Falls killed in the war. (Stanley was killed in October 1917 and Hedley was killed with the Canadians in August 1918. The Goodyears are the subject of an excellent family history, *The Danger Tree* by David Macfarlane, Macfarlane, Walter & Ross, 1991.) Mortally wounded in the attack was Second Lieutenant Samuel Ebsary, whose brother, Hubert had been killed in Gallipoli. The long casualty lists continued to haunt the families of Newfoundland.

By Battle of the Somme standards October 12th, 1916 was a reasonable success, such were the horrors of that infamous battle.

The Caribou Memorial was erected on the furthest point reached by the Newfoundland Regiment on October 12th, 1916. Remnants of the German trench system run through this small park. It gives a commanding view of the battlefield.

Return to your car and continue east on the D11 over the A1 Motorway until you reach the N17. Turn left for Bapaume, and continue through it, on to Arras, 30 km distant.

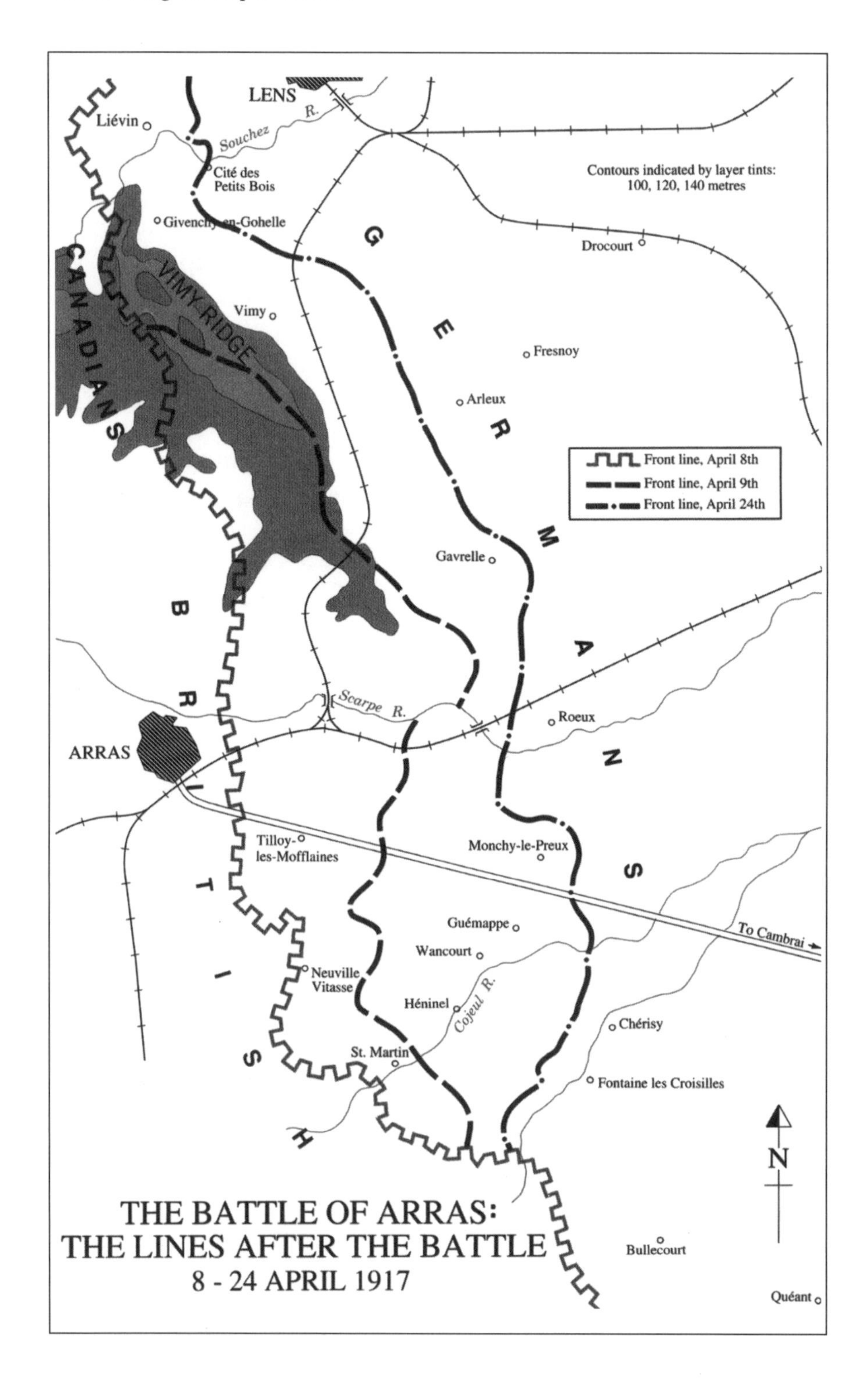
LENS
Liévin
Souchez R.
Cité des Petits Bois
Givenchy-en-Gohelle
VIMY RIDGE
Vimy
CANADIANS
GERMANS
BRITISH
Contours indicated by layer tints: 100, 120, 140 metres
Drocourt
Fresnoy
Arleux
Front line, April 8th
Front line, April 9th
Front line, April 24th
Gavrelle
Scarpe R.
Roeux
ARRAS
Tilloy-les-Mofflaines
Monchy-le-Preux
Guémappe
Wancourt
To Cambrai
Neuville Vitasse
Héninel
Cojeul R.
Chérisy
St. Martin
Fontaine les Croisilles
N
Bullecourt
Quéant
THE BATTLE OF ARRAS:
THE LINES AFTER THE BATTLE
8 - 24 APRIL 1917

Historical Overview
The First Battle of the Scarpe, April 9th-14th, 1917

The Newfoundland Regiment after the Somme

During the month of January 1917 the 1st Battalion, the Newfoundland Regiment, spent much of its time training and assimilating new recruits. By the end of the month they were back in the line near Gueudecourt. In February British forces probed the enemy's lines and they found that the Germans were gradually withdrawing from the old Somme battlefield. Elated by this news the generals decided to put pressure on the retreating Huns. Through February and March the Newfoundlanders participated in this pursuit and fought several minor actions against the German rearguards. Their most significant encounter took place at Sailly-Saillisel, March1st-3rd, 1917.

Although the British inflicted many casualties on the enemy as they retreated, the Germans were, nonetheless successful in withdrawing 80 km to a well prepared defence system, known as the Hindenburg line. By doing this they shortened their front freeing up thousands of troops. This withdrawal was considered an Allied victory, as a substantial piece of occupied France was now liberated.

On March 28th, 1917 the 29th Division was ordered to Arras to take part in the upcoming offensive.

The First Battle of the Scarpe, April 9th-14th, 1917

Before the dead of the Battle of the Somme had been buried, the French and British Generals had decided on another Offensive. It was to be a massive two-pronged attack by the French and British armies. The British would open the offensive against the German positions, east of Arras, including the impregnable Vimy Ridge. The French, attacking a week later, would strike the German lines, along the Chemin des Dames, 200 km east of Paris. The combined forces, incorporating new tactics, would strike the mortal blow to the Kaiser's armies.

The British attack planned for 20 Divisions; 400,000 men, to assault on a 20 km front, north and south of the Scarpe river. British artillery would fire more than two million shells to soften up the enemy's trench systems. The sheer weight of men and munitions was a guarantee of success. However the plan held many similarities to the plan that failed so desperately on July 1st, 1916.

North of the Scarpe river the strongest German position was Vimy Ridge, and south of the river the most dominant height was that of Monchy-le-Preux. For the attack to succeed both heights would have to fall.

The attack south of the Scarpe was to utilize seven infantry divisions in the initial assault. The 29th Division, including the 1st Battalion, The Newfoundland Regiment, was allocated the task of supporting the first wave, however and wherever it was required.

The Battle Opens

At 5:20 a.m. on April 9th, 1917 the Battle of Arras was launched. Following behind a week-long artillery bombardment, which launched more than two million shells on the German positions, the British infantry swarmed across No Man's Land, sweeping the enemy out of his positions. North of the Scarpe river the Canadians seized most of Vimy Ridge and to the south British Divisions were equally successful, advancing three km.

On April 10th the attack continued, and against stiffening resistance British Divisions pushed forward a further two km. It was clear however that the Germans were unwilling to yield more ground and were fiercely counter-attacking each British advance. Still in support, the 29th Division watched and anticipated their call to action.

The most significant position south of the Scarpe was the village of Monchy-le-Preux, sitting atop the highest and most dominant ridge in the battle area. Both sides, understanding its importance raced their men towards Monchy. On April 11th the 37th British Division fought its way into the village. In the face of heavy artillery fire they took and held Monchy. The 3rd British Cavalry Division reinforced the 37th, but German machine-guns took a heavy toll on both mounts and riders. The day had not gone well south of the Scarpe. The capture of Monchy was the only tangible gain and more than 8,000 men had been lost. The attacking divisions were exhausted and the Germans were fighting back with great determination. The great advance had lost its momentum.

On April 12th the 29th Division was ordered to relieve the troops in Monchy and to continue the attack. However it was found that the units in the line were too disorganized to launch the attack immediately and it was postponed until April 14th.

After the fighting of April 11th Monchy was the most easterly position captured by the British. It was in a sharp salient, one km deep, surrounded on three sides by the Germans. It was in an incredibly vulnerable position and when an attack was ordered which would only deepen the salient few could have thought it was the correct thing to do. In the confusion not enough men could be in place for the attack so in the end only two battalions, roughly 1,300 men, would participate. They were the 1st Battalion, The Essex Regiment and the 1st Battalion, The Newfoundland Regiment. The same two battalions that attacked at Beaumont-Hamel on July 1st, 1916.

The plan was to attack from the eastern edge of the village, behind a creeping barrage, capture the German front line and push on to Infantry Hill (Hill 100), a total advance of 1,000 metres. Included in the objectives were a number of German strong-points near the village. It sounded so simple.

At 5:30 a.m. the barrage opened and the Newfoundlanders started their advance. Immediately they encountered machine-gun fire, and although taking casualties, continued to advance to the German trench. They found it deserted. Without hesitation, they pushed on to Infantry Hill. Within two hours both the Essex and the Newfoundland Regiment had succeeded in taking their objectives. The Newfoundlanders busily began consolidating their gains in Machine-Gun Wood and on Infantry Hill.

What they did not know was that the enemy were employing a new style of defence. They had only lightly manned their front line and had withdrawn their men back so they could be utilized in a rapid counter-attack. After 8 a.m. Newfoundlanders in the new positions could see Germans collecting on their flanks and shortly thereafter the assault was made. Behind an effective artillery fire the enemy quickly moved in a pincer formation cutting the men off from the village. Many tried to get back to Monchy but were shot down as they crossed the open ground. Others were overwhelmed on Infantry Hill by superior numbers of Huns. Within an hour it was over. The British attack had failed and the Germans began advancing on the undefended village of Monchy.

In Monchy the Battalion's Commanding Officer, Lieutenant-Colonel J. Forbes-Robertson could not determine the progress of the battle as all communication with the front was cut. Wounded stragglers made their way into the village and told him of the catastrophic events. Even as they talked German artillery fire was pasting the village and their infantry were rapidly approaching. Forbes-Robertson took every man he could find and moved to the trench on the eastern edge of Monchy. There, he and eight others made an historic stand. The small group created so much fire that it discouraged the enemy and kept him pinned down. Not realizing what a small force opposed them, the Germans did not press the attack. In the late afternoon a number of reinforcements reached Forbes-Robertson. But he and his band had to hold on until they were relieved at 8 p.m. that night.*

The day had gone very badly for both the Essex and the Newfoundlanders. Between them they had lost: killed, wounded and prisoners more than 1,000 men of an attacking force of roughly 1,300. The 1st Battalion, The Newfoundland Regiment lost 166 dead, 141 wounded and 150 taken prisoner. For the second time in the war the Newfoundland Regiment had been wiped out.

The Newfoundlanders were not yet finished with the Arras Offensive. On April 23rd, 1917 they played a supporting role in the Second Battle of the Scarpe. It was another futile attack where the British forces attempted to advance south of the Scarpe. This time the remnants of the Essex and Newfoundland Regiments only had to hold their line, but even then The Regiment lost 63 men.

The Battle of Arras continued officially until May 15th, 1917. Like so many battles it had started with much promise, only to be drowned in the mud and blood of the Western Front. Total British losses, including Newfoundlanders, South Africans, Canadians and Australians totalled 150,000, killed, wounded and missing.

* *The saviours of Monchy were: Lieutenant-Colonel James Forbes-Robertson, DSO, Corporal Albert Rose, MM, Sergeant Walter Pitcher, MM (killed at Masnieres, November 20th, 1917), Lieutenant Kevin Keagan, MC, Sergeant Charles Parsons, MM, Sergeant Ross Waterfield, MM (killed October 9th, 1917), Private Frederick Curran, Corporal J.H. Hillier, MM and Private Japheth Hounsell, MM (killed April 13th, 1918), all of the Newfoundland Regiment. The last man was Private V.M. Parsons of the Essex Regiment.*

Forbes-Robertson won the Victoria Cross in April 1918. (He was born Cheltenham, U.K., July 7th, 1884; died Bourton-on-the-Water, U.K., August 5th, 1955.)

Private Bernard Ryan
Killed in action April 14th, 1917.
Buried Cagnicourt British Cemetery,
III.A.19.

Corporal James R. Tuff
St. John's. Age 22.
Died of wounds received at Monchy, April
28th, 1917.
Buried Duisans British Cemetery, III.H.17.

Company Sergeant Major Athur J. Penny
Trinity Bay. Age 25.
Killed in action April 14th, 1917.
Commemorated on the Beaumont-Hamel
Memorial.

Private William J. Neville
St. John's. Age 20.
Killed in action April 14th, 1917.
Commemorated on the Beaumont-Hamel
Memorial.

The Caribou at Monchy. (N. Christie)

The Tour - Monchy-le-Preux, April 14th, 1917

Leave Arras on the south-east following the road to Cambrai (D939). After three km you reach the village of Tilloy-les-Mofflaines. The village was in German hands on April 9th, 1917, but was quickly captured by British troops. Two km further on you reach a round-about. Turn left on the D37 to Feuchy. Turn right after 100 metres and drive through an industrial park continuing east over the Motorway and past Monchy British Cemetery. The village of Monchy-le-Preux is one km directly ahead of you. Continue into Monchy until you are in the village. The first monument that appears on your left is a memorial to the 37th Division. In stiff fighting they captured the village on April 11th, 1917. Less than 200 metres further on is the Newfoundland Memorial Caribou. The Memorial was built on top of a German bunker.

There is not much to be seen in Monchy as the views are blocked by the houses. In 1917 the village had been devastated by the artillery of both sides. The area was also the scene of fierce fighting by the 3rd Cavalry Division and the bodies of their horses were scattered in and around the village.

Follow the road descending to the south-east, passing just south of the Mairie (Town Hall) and exit the village. Once clear of the village continue 500 metres until a rough paved road (running east) appears on your left. This junction was the location of the Windmill, part of the German front line. Park your car. Walk (or drive but be careful of the mud) 400 metres down the rough road.

Point One; East of Monchy, April 14th, 1917

Looking north from this position you can see the entire battlefield of April 14th, 1917. To orient yourself the jump-off position of the Essex and Newfoundlanders was on the eastern edge of the village, facing due east. The opposing German trench was only 250 metres away. Infantry Hill or Hill 100, the main objective of the attack is 700 metres north-east of you. Bois du Vert, where some of the German reserves were held is one km east of you. The village beyond that is Boiry-Notre Dame, three km distant. The small wood 200 metres south was known as Machine Gun Wood in 1917. It was a German strong-point.

At 5:30 a.m. on April 14th, 1917 the area all around you would have exploded in smoke and fire as the British barrage peppered the German

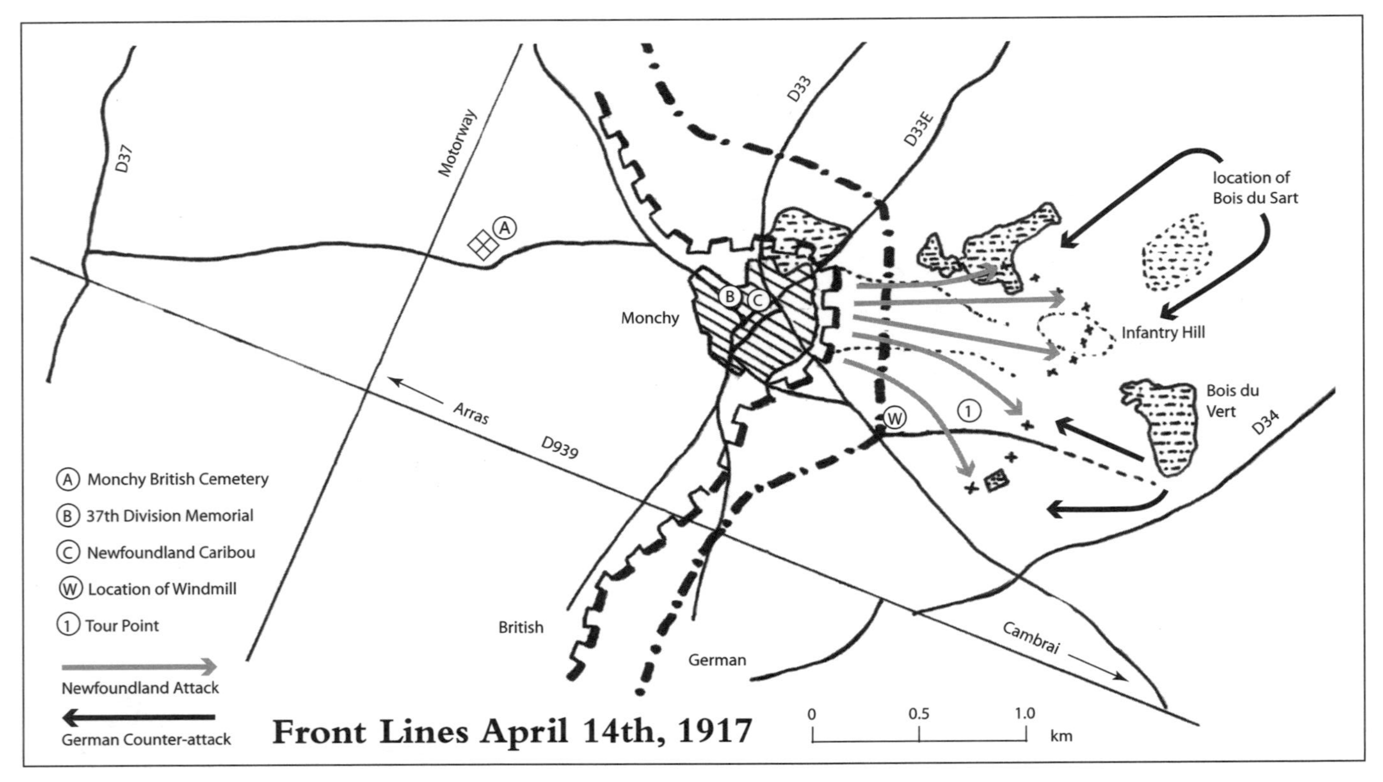

The Battle of Arras, 1917.

View towards Infantry Hill from the Windmill. (N. Christie)

View towards Monchy from the Windmill. (N. Christie)

The Monchy Caribou, circa 1925. (Compare to page 58.) (PANF)

positions. The Newfoundlanders would have left their trenches on the eastern edge of the village. Within minutes they would have crossed 250 metres of No Man's Land and entered the enemy's front line. Shortly after groups of Newfoundlanders would have been seen advancing across the fields 700 metres north of you and on to Infantry Hill. Another group crossed the fields directly at you, passing through the point on which you are standing, advancing to Machine Gun Wood, 200 metres south of you. This whole action took place in less than one hour. The men would then have been digging in.

The Germans reacted quickly to the advance and they began massing troops in the Bois du Vert, 900 metres east of you. The enemy gradually started moving forward, swarming towards and around the Newfoundlanders. In conjunction with effective artillery fire, they cut off and destroyed the small groups, killing or capturing the soldiers holding Infantry Hill and Machine Gun wood.

Some men tried to retreat back to Monchy but were cut down by superior German fire. By 10 a.m. the attack was over.

Now from a German perspective, the victorious soldiers slowly started to move towards Monchy. The village itself was being heavily bombarded. The Germans, unsure how strongly it was held, hesitated, which allowed Lieutenant-Colonel Forbes-Robertson and his small band the chance to get to the trench on the eastern edge of the village and open fire. They raised an effective fire so disproportionate to their numbers that the first waves of Germans were shot down in the open fields. The enemy was so deceived by the fire that they never made the full out attack that surely would have overwhelmed the handful of men holding them up. By 8 p.m. the battlefield, littered with dead Germans and Newfoundlanders, was quiet.

Return to your car and continue on the road until you reach the D34 after one km. Turn right on the D34 until you reach the D939 (500 metres). Turn right to return to Arras.

To visit the Masnieres Caribou, turn left on the D939 towards Cambrai (for directions refer to page 71).

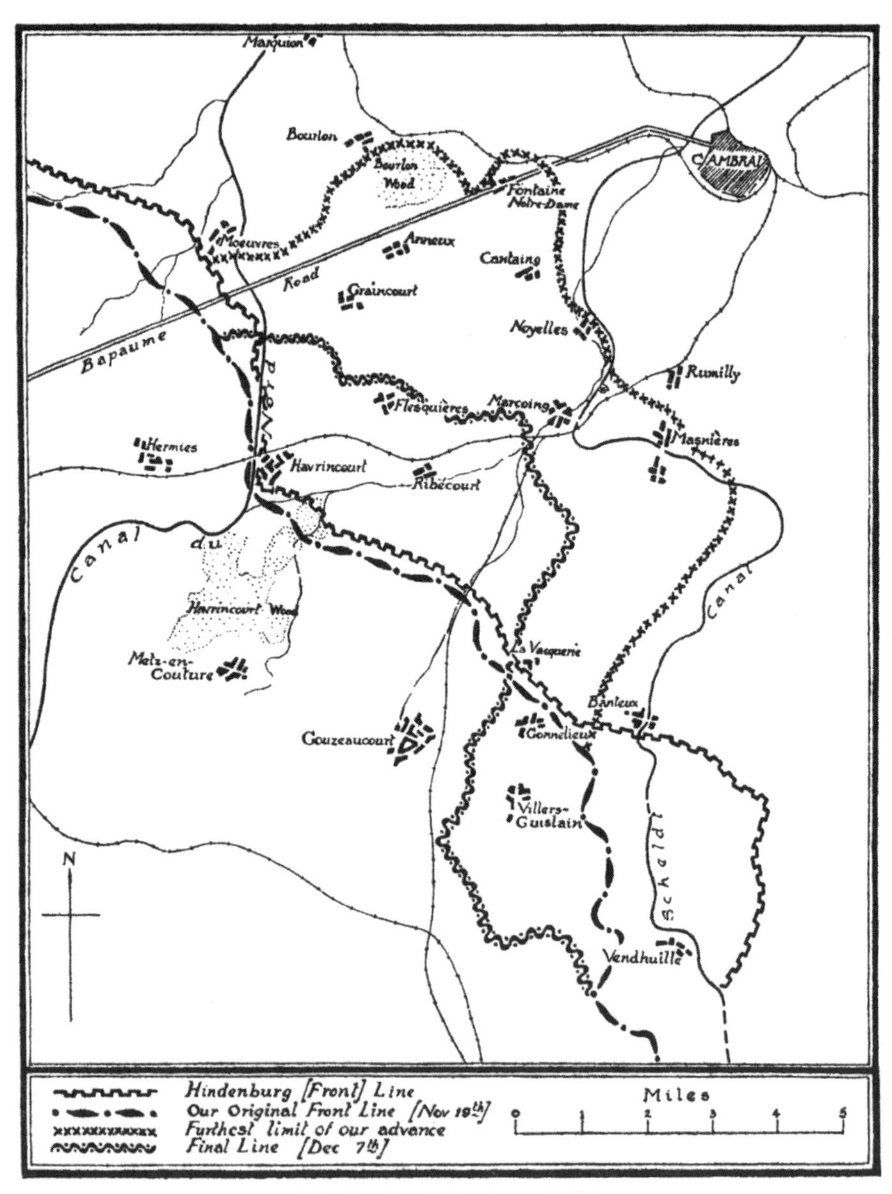

The Battle of Cambrai, 1917.

Historical Overview
The Battle of Cambrai
November 20th - December 7th, 1917

The Newfoundlanders after Monchy

After their disastrous attack at Monchy on April 14th, 1917, the Newfoundlanders had once again to be reinforced and retrained. Like so many British units in the bloody fighting at Arras, they had only a brief respite before being committed once again to another ferocious offensive. This time it was the Third Battle of Ypres or Passchendaele as the entire offensive became to be known.

Third Ypres opened on July 31st, 1917. In the first days of fighting British troops advanced three km against a strong enemy defensive line. But over the next few days the weather turned against the attackers and heavy rain turned the battlefield into a sea of mud delaying further attacks. On August 16th the offensive was renewed. The Battle of Langemarck was to involve 16 British Divisions attacking across the Ypres Salient. The task given to the men of the 29th Division was to capture the ground west of the infamous village of Langemarck.

The Newfoundlanders were to support the 29th's main assault and despite the heavy rain and German shell-fire they advanced 1,500 metres and took their objectives at a meagre cost of 103 casualties. The attack of the 29th Division was the only real success in an otherwise dismal day for the British.

The Newfoundland Regiment was not through with Ypres. On October 9th, 1917 the 29th Division was one of 13 Divisions that took part in the Battle of Poelcapelle. The attack took place over a 10 km front with the 29th Division assaulting on the left flank of the offensive. By this time conditions on the battlefield had deteriorated further, but none-the-less the Newfoundlanders and their British comrades advanced two km through knee-deep mud. Fierce German counter-attacks drove them back 200 metres, but they held on to most of their gains. Once again it was the 29th Division that provided the only victory on another day of disaster. This success only added more laurels to the reputation of the "incomparable" 29th Division. October 9th, 1917 resulted in another 127 men of the Newfoundland Battalion being killed or wounded. Amongst the fallen was Lieutenant Stanley Goodyear, MC. His brother, Oswald had been killed at Gueudecourt and within a year a second brother, Hedley, would also die on the battlefield.

Shortly after the Battle of Poelcapelle the Newfoundlanders were withdrawn from the front and started training for a new offensive. For the first time tanks were added to the infantry exercises. Few had ever seen a tank although most knew them by reputation. By October 17th The Regiment was ordered to a new sector of the front. The men did not know that they were about to be part of one of the most historic battles in military history.

The Battle of Cambrai, 1917

1917 had been a bleak year for the Allies. It had a promising start in April with the initial success of the Battle of Arras, but after April 9th, 1917 it was all down hill. The later stages of the battle had floundered with heavy losses. The French offensive had failed and resulted in mutiny. Russia had surrendered, the Bolsheviks took power, Italy had been hammered at Caporetto and the Battle of Passchendaele had cost hundreds of thousands of casualties with very little gain. The morale of the Allies was at its lowest point in the War.

But failure had produced one positive change. Sir Julian Byng, the former Commander of the Canadian Corps, was placed in Command of the British Third Army. Byng was an unusual man, results-oriented and open to new ideas. His Third Army had not been involved in any major attacks since May 1917. It was fresh and ready.

Byng's staff had developed a modern concept for the First World War. They proposed using the new innovation of the tanks, in mass formation, over an area where the ground conditions were good and to capture a specific, strategic target. In addition he would employ the element of surprise. There would be no massive preliminary bombardment to warn the Germans. His Third Army would create a breakthrough and the cavalry would exploit it to their fullest capability. It is difficult to say whether or not the disasters of 1917 had weakened the obstinacy of his superiors; however, Byng did gain approval for his project.

His strategic target was Cambrai, a vital supply centre for the Germans. His plan called for tanks and infantry to breach the Hindenburg line south-west of Cambrai, seizing the canal crossings south of the city, and capturing the dominating heights of Bourlon Wood. By capturing Bourlon Byng's Divisions would control the Arras-Cambrai road. This would cut-off the German Divisions on the Arras front and perhaps force a withdrawal. To achieve his victory Byng would employ 278 tanks of the Tank Corps and 6 infantry Divisions trained in tactics to operate in cooperation with the tanks.

The chosen battlefield was sound as this part of the Hindenburg line was known to be weakly held. It was also open ground, undamaged by warfare and conducive to the movement of his tanks. Byng also knew he had only two days to exploit any success before masses of German reinforcements would arrive. So the attackers must exploit their opportunities quickly. Once through the Hindenburg Line there would be no time to lose.

One of the reserve divisions designated for the attack was the 29th, and it included the 1st Battalion, The Newfoundland Regiment.

The Objectives of the 29th Division

South-west of Cambrai the Hindenburg line was three km deep and consisted of three trench systems; a series of strong outpost lines, the main trench system and a support line. Each was a well-entrenched position, protected by belts of barbed wire. Three km behind it was another system, known as the Hindenburg Reserve line. Byng's total force totalled 17 infantry and four cavalry divisions.

The objectives of the 29th Division were to follow on the main attack, take the villages of Marcoing, Masinieres, push over the St.Quentin (Escaut) canal, and capture the Masnieres-Beaurevoir line (the Hindenburg Reserve line). Once the objectives were taken the cavalry would continue the drive on Cambrai. The Newfoundland Battalion was to be part of the force to seize the St. Quentin canal.

On Tuesday morning of November 20th, 1917 at 6:20 a.m. a new era of warfare was born. Behind a barrage of 1,000 guns Byng's troops and tanks quickly overran the Hindenburg line. The surprise had been achieved. At 10 a.m. the 29th Division began their advance. Accompanied by four tanks the infantry, including the Newfoundlanders, moved through the former German lines and over Welsh Ridge. Before long the four tanks were knocked out and the men were encountering enemy machine-gun fire. They quickly overcame the opposition and shortly were through the Hindenburg Support line and into open country. Before them they could see the Escaut river valley and their objectives, Marcoing and Masinieres, two km away.

The soldiers descended into the river valley and covered the two km easily, with few casualties. As they approached Marcoing Wood, the Germans opened fire from Masnieres and Les Rues Vertes. They continued to the canal and probing the enemy line the Newfoundlanders crossed the lock and in the face of machine-gun fire, rushed to the railway track. Their advance was held up as Masnieres was still in German hands, although Marcoing had already fallen to the men of the 29th Division. (To make matters worse for the tanks one of the few bridges they could use to get across the canal had been damaged and then collapsed when a tank tried to cross it.) Snipers and machine-guns took their toll as the ranks of the Newfoundland Regiment grew thinner, but they had secured the canal crossing. In the afternoon the Newfoundlanders attacked down the banks of the canal towards Masnieres. At 4 p.m. the first of the cavalry arrived. The Fort Garry Horse of the Canadian Cavalry Brigade, were the only cavalry to get across the canal and push towards Cambrai.*

At nightfall the battlefield was quiet. The first day had gone well for the British and the Newfoundlanders. They had advanced six km. These successes were enough to set bells pealing all across Britain. The breakthrough was at hand.

On November 21st, 1917 the Newfoundlanders continued the attack on Masinieres and finally most of the village fell. But it was clear the Germans had recovered from their initial shock and were now yielding very little ground. The problem facing the attackers was that they did not have enough men to take the Masnieres-Beaurevoir line. The impetus of their attack was waning due to a lack of reserves. They were no longer strong enough to take the German positions.

The Newfoundland Regiment lost a few of its characters on the 21st. Sergeant Walter Pitcher, MM, one of the saviours of Monchy was killed, as was a Battalion sniper, an Inuit, John Shiwak. Shiwak was one of the very few "Eskimos" serving (He is commemorated on the Beaumont-Hamel Memorial.).

* *One squadron of the Fort Garry Horse got across the canal at Masnieres and under the command of Lieutenant Harcus Strachan attacked and captured an enemy battery. Strachan was awarded the Victoria Cross. Harcus Strachan, VC, MC was born at West Lothian, Scotland, November 7th, 1884; he died at Vancouver, British Columbia, May 1st, 1982.*

The fighting thus far had cost Newfoundland 248 men, including 53 dead. The survivors were withdrawn to Marcoing for a rest.

The Battle south of Cambrai had gone reasonably well but the attacks west of Cambrai had encountered some difficulty and they were not advancing on schedule. German resistance at Bourlon Wood was especially problematic and this fortified position could not be taken.

On November 23rd the British continued their attacks on Bourlon Wood, but could not win a clear victory. By November 28th the offensive was spent. Although they had won a lot of territory, they had won only a small piece of ground east of the St. Quentin canal. It had been taken by the 29th Division.

On the morning of November 30th, 1917 the Germans tried to retake their lost territory. Behind a crushing barrage, 9 German Divisions counterattacked; four attacked from the south-east, behind the British position at Masnieres. The Newfoundlanders were in billets in Marcoing when the attack was launched and they quickly moved out to Marcoing Copse, east of the village, to meet the German onslaught. They were unaware that the Germans were advancing on a wide front behind them, and had already advanced more than one km. The men of the 29th Division, in fact the entire British force was dangerously close to being cut off. In fact the British command was throwing all available troops into battle, including a handful of American Engineers. Even the last of the tanks were being brought back into action.

In probably their most critical fight of the war the men of the Newfoundland Regiment fought with such tenacity and courage that not only did they stop the Germans, but drove them back, establishing a defensive position east of Marcoing Wood. They prevented the enemy from cutting off their comrades holding on in Masnieres and north of the St. Quentin canal. By their actions the Newfoundlanders helped save the day.

The fighting was severe all along the British positions. The Germans retook Bourlon Wood, and it seemed that all the Cambrai gains would be lost. But British infantry, cavalry and tanks through pure determination, managed to stop the enemy and even regain some of the lost positions.

The fighting continued on December 1st. In their positions south of the canal the Newfoundlanders suffered in the face of artillery and machine-gun fire. Snipers also claimed their victims and one of them was Lieutenant Arthur Herder. His brother Hubert had been killed leading the attack at Beaumont-Hamel on July 1st, 1916. At this time the British command took the precaution of evacuating their surviving soldiers from Masnieres and Les Rues Vertes. On December 3rd, after facing another German onslaught the Newfoundlanders were withdrawn and their positions left to the enemy.

The Battle of Cambrai officially ended on December 7th, 1917. The net gain of the original advance was negated by the area lost to the German counter-offensive. Essentially Cambrai was a draw. It had cost the British 38,000 killed and wounded and 6,000 prisoners. Once again the optimism of another great breakthrough had been washed away by a stinging reverse. It had been a "cruel disappointment." Cambrai did launch a new era in warfare but sadly it's lessons would not be utilized until the Second World War (and then by the Germans).

For the valiant Newfoundlanders the battle had been a costly one. Since the battle opened on November 20th until they withdrew on December 3rd the Battalion had lost 462 men, including more than 100 killed. But for the Newfoundland Regiment the defence of Masnieres was their greatest military feat of arms in the entire war. In recognition of their actions the King honoured the Newfoundland Regiment, by authorizing the prefix "Royal" to their title. In the entire First World War the Newfoundlanders were the only unit to be so honoured.

The Tour - Masnieres, November 20th -December 3rd, 1917

There are two routes to Masnieres; one is through the battlefields of the First World War, the other is more direct. Have your map handy when following these instructions.

Leave Arras by the south-east following the road to Cambrai, N939. Follow the N939, past Tilloy-les-Mofflaines (2 km), Monchy-le-Preux (this is the point where the Monchy Tour and the Masnieres Tour meet), Vis-en-Artois (12 km), over the Canal du Nord to Marquion (22 km).

On the eastern outskirts of the village turn right (south) on the D15. As you drive south you will see the profile of Bourlon Wood on your left. Continue on the D15 past Bourlon, across the N30 (7 km from Marquion), over the A2-E19 Motorway, to Trescault (14 km from Marquion). Continue through Trescault on the D15 to Gouzeaucourt (4 km). In Gouzeaucourt turn right at the 'T' junction, driving into the village . After 400 metres turn left on the D917 towards Bonavis and Masnieres.

You are driving on one of the access roads used by the tanks and infantry going to the front on November 20th, 1917. Gouzeaucourt was also the scene of heavy fighting in the German counter-offensive on November 30th. It was lost early in the morning and retaken by the Guards Division in the afternoon.

After three km you are driving through what was the outpost line of the Hindenburg system. The village of La Vacquerie to your left was woven into the German front line. One km further on the main Hindenburg line cut across the road. As you pass over the A26 Motorway you can see a long ridge 1.5 km over to your left, this is Welsh Ridge and the route taken by the Newfoundlanders on November 20th. (The Ridge can be reached via La Vacquerie, following a rough road running north-east of the village.) The Hindenburg Support line cut the D917 1.5 km further on. This area was quickly captured by tanks and infantry on November 20th. It was also captured and held by the Germans on November 30th.

At Bonavis (two km) keep left on the N44 to Masnieres. The view as you descend into the Escaut river valley is exceptional. Before you unfolds the Battle of Cambrai's southern battlefield. The village directly ahead is Masnieres (4 km) and Marcoing is clearly visible

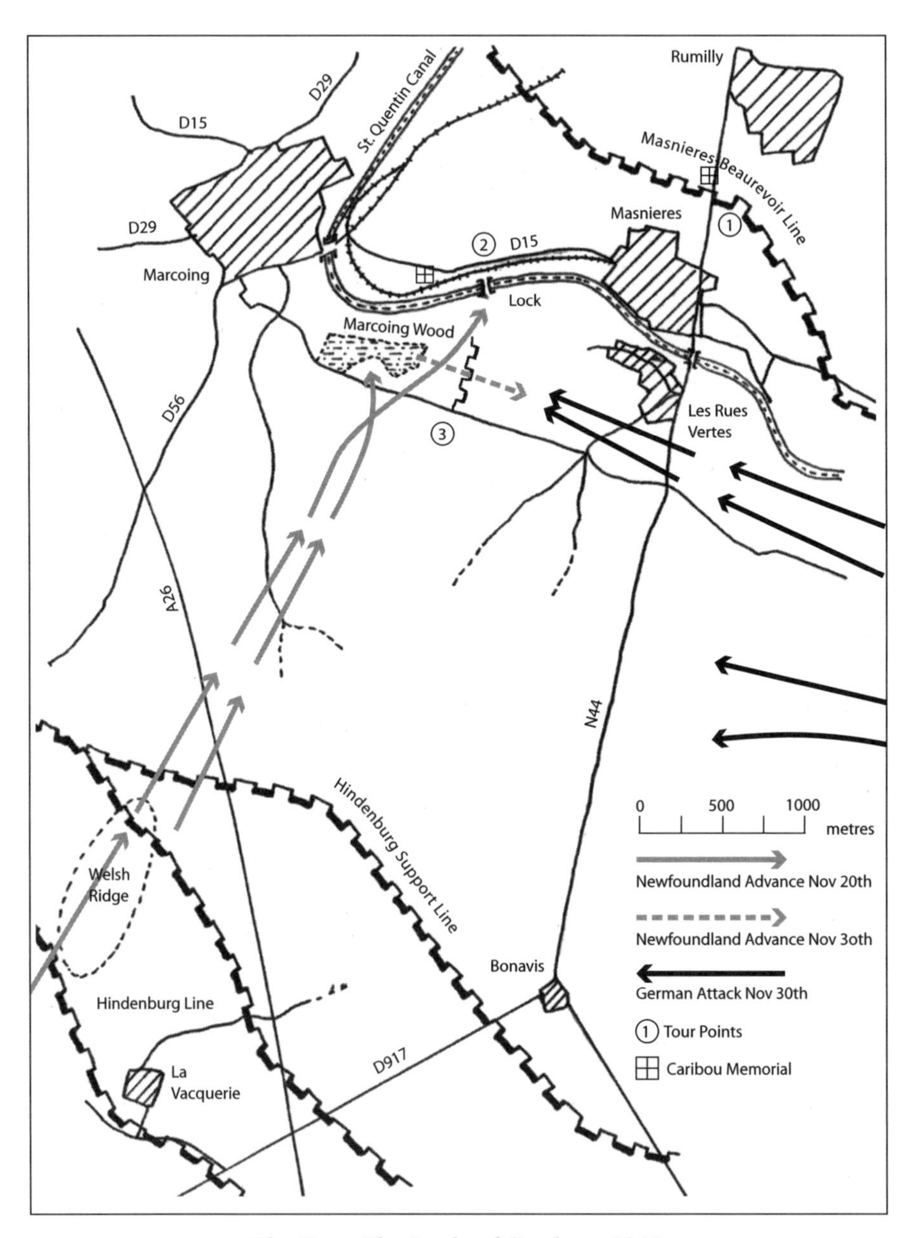

The Tour; The Battle of Cambrai, 1917.

on the canal/river bend west of Masnieres. You may want to stop to get a clear orientation. The village south of the canal/river is Les Rues Vertes (now part of Masnieres), pass through it and continue over the canal. The bridge you are passing over was the one the British tank collapsed on November 20th, 1917. Continue through the village on the N44 towards Rumilly and Cambrai. The Newfoundland Memorial appears on your left 600 metres outside of Masnieres. Stop your car and proceed to the Memorial.

A more direct route***: Take the D939 from Arras to Cambrai. Keep right through the city, following the direction to St. Quentin and Peronne. Take the N44 south out of Cambrai to Rumilly and Masnieres. After six km the Newfoundland Memorial appears on your right.***

Point One: The Masnieres Caribou

The Newfoundland Memorial is located on what was part of the Masnieres-Beaurevoir line and the furthest point reached by the British in this sector during the Battle of Cambrai. It is easy to see why the Germans chose this position. Looking back you can see the spires of Cambrai and, down the road, how it dominates the village of Masnieres and the critically important bridge across the canal. Although the view is obscured at times by trees and houses, one can clearly imagine the fighting that took place as the British infantry and tanks fought to penetrate these positions. It was in this area that the Fort Garry Horse made their attack on the German battery. Their horses were shot down, but the men managed to inflict a few casualties, take a few prisoners and get back to the British lines. It was quite an achievement.

Return to your car and follow the N44 into Masnieres. Once in the village turn right on the D15 to Marcoing. Continue on the D15 out of Masnieres. After 1.2 km a small road on your left appears. It is the 100 metre long access road to the canal lock (Ecl. de Bracheux) where the Newfoundlanders made their heroic charge on November 20th. Follow the road down to the lock.

Point Two: The Attack of November 20th, 1917.

On the morning of November 20th, the Regiment had succeeded in crossing the Hindenburg Support system with few casualties. There were pockets of resistance, but in general it was an easy advance. They

The Masnieres Caribou, circa 1924. (PANF)

moved quickly capturing Marcoing Wood. However when they neared the canal they found that Masnieres and Les Rues Vertes were still in German hands and the enemy was firing into their flank. The most important job for them was to get across the St. Quentin canal. The canal itself was too wide and deep so the Newfoundlanders made their assault over the canal lock. Led by Captain Paterson and assisted by a tank, which fired at the Germans covering the lock, the men made it across and into the buildings near where you stand. The Germans had machine-gun positions on the railway that were inflicting many casualties. Once again the attackers took the initiative and rushed the enemy's posts. In a brief fight the railway was cleared.

(The dead of this action were collected together by the Catholic Chaplain of the Regiment, Tom Nangle, and given an honoured burial. After the war 24 Newfoundland graves were exhumed and reburied in Marcoing British Cemetery. To visit the cemetery return to the D15, turn left for Marcoing and the cemetery appears 500 metres further down the D15 on the south side of the road.)

The men turned their attention on Marcoing and discovered that it had already been taken. However their assistance was required in Masnieres, where the Germans were putting up a stiff fight. The Newfoundlanders advanced between the D15 and the canal into Masnieres. The Newfoundlanders fought in the village on November 20th and 21st, assisting other men of the 29th Division in driving the Germans out. Shelling and snipers took a heavy toll. Amongst those killed here was a Regimental sniper John Shiwak, a Labrador "Eskimo". He was buried in the village but after the war his grave could not be found. On November 22nd, the 1st Battalion, The Newfoundland Regiment was withdrawn from the line into Marcoing village. They remained there until November 30th.

Return to your car and drive back to the D15. Turn right for Masnieres.

Once in the village turn right on the N44, drive over the bridge and through the subdivision that was known as Les Rues Vertes. On the outskirts of Les Rues Vertes you come to a 4-way crossroads. Take the unnumbered road on your right going towards Marcoing. Follow the road through a round-about and after 1.2 km stop by a farm track on your right.

The lock over which the Newfoundllanders crossed the Canal, November 20th, 1917.
(N. Christie)

View from Caribou towards Cambrai (on the horizon). (N. Christie)

Point Three: Counter-Attack, November 30th-December 3rd, 1917

The place where you are standing comes into play twice during the battle. It was through this position that the Newfoundlanders descended from the ridges south of you. They had cleared the Hindenburg Support line and had walked two km over open ground. Marcoing Copse would have been 300 metres west of you (very little of the Copse remains). It is also at this point that they encountered German machine-gun fire from Les Rues Vertes and made their dash for the canal, crossing over the lock.

More importantly it was where they made their gallant and strategic stand against the German counter-attack on November 30th, 1917. The men were in billets in Marcoing 1.5 km west of you, when the Germans launched their counter-stroke. They had no way of knowing the extent of the enemy attack nor did they appreciate their predicament. The Germans had launched a two-pronged attack with the intent of pinching off the British forces. The early success of the Battle of Cambrai had created a deep salient and now the Germans were attacking the flanks of that salient.

By the time the orders were received in Marcoing the Germans had broken through the British left flank and advanced 7 km, and held positions south of Masnieres. One more successful thrust and the 29th Division would be surrounded. As the Newfoundlanders raced from the village to Marcoing Copse they found the Germans were already there. In a distinguished action they met the attacking enemy and drove him back, finally establishing a north-south defensive line in the field in front of you. Here they held on, allowing British troops trapped in Masnieres to escape.

Holding the line was a desperate affair. The Germans wanted to close the ring on the British. However resistance here and near Bourlon in the north was preventing the enemy from succeeding.

The Germans shelled the Newfoundlander positions continuously through December 1st, and inflicted many casualties, but the line held. There was to be no respite through December 2nd and 3rd. Casualties mounted in the face of heavy artillery fire, but it appeared the Germans had enough of the fight themselves and there was no major infantry assault. On the night of December 3rd, 1917 the 1st Battalion, The Royal Newfoundland Regiment was relieved. For them the Battle of Cambrai was over.

Private George Kane
St. John's. Age 24.
Killed in action December 3rd, 1917.
Commemorated on the Beaumont-Hamel Memorial.

Second Lieutenant Walter M. Greene, DCM
Cape Broyle. Age 24.
Killed in action November 20th, 1917.
Buried Marcoing British Cemetery, II.E.10.

Private Hugh P. Bowden, MM
Bay Roberts. Age 21.
Killed in action November 20th, 1917.
Buried Marcoing British Cemetery, II.G.1.

Lieutenant George Langmead
St. John's. Age 23.
Died of wounds December 8th, 1917.
Buried Rocquigny-Equancourt Road British Cemetery, VIII.B.29.

In these fields 57 Newfoundlanders were killed between November 30th and December 3rd. The graves of 54 were never found or never identified. Once again Newfoundland had paid dearly for their place in history.

The line they had held so dearly was left to the Germans when the British Command realized that they could not hold all their gains. When the Battle of Cambrai ended officially on December 7th, 1917, despite the early successes, it had been a stand-off with virtually no territorial advantage to either side.

Return to your car and retrace your route back to Arras.

The grave of Private Stephen Fortune in Marcoing British Cemetery. He was killed November 22nd 1917.

(N. Christie)

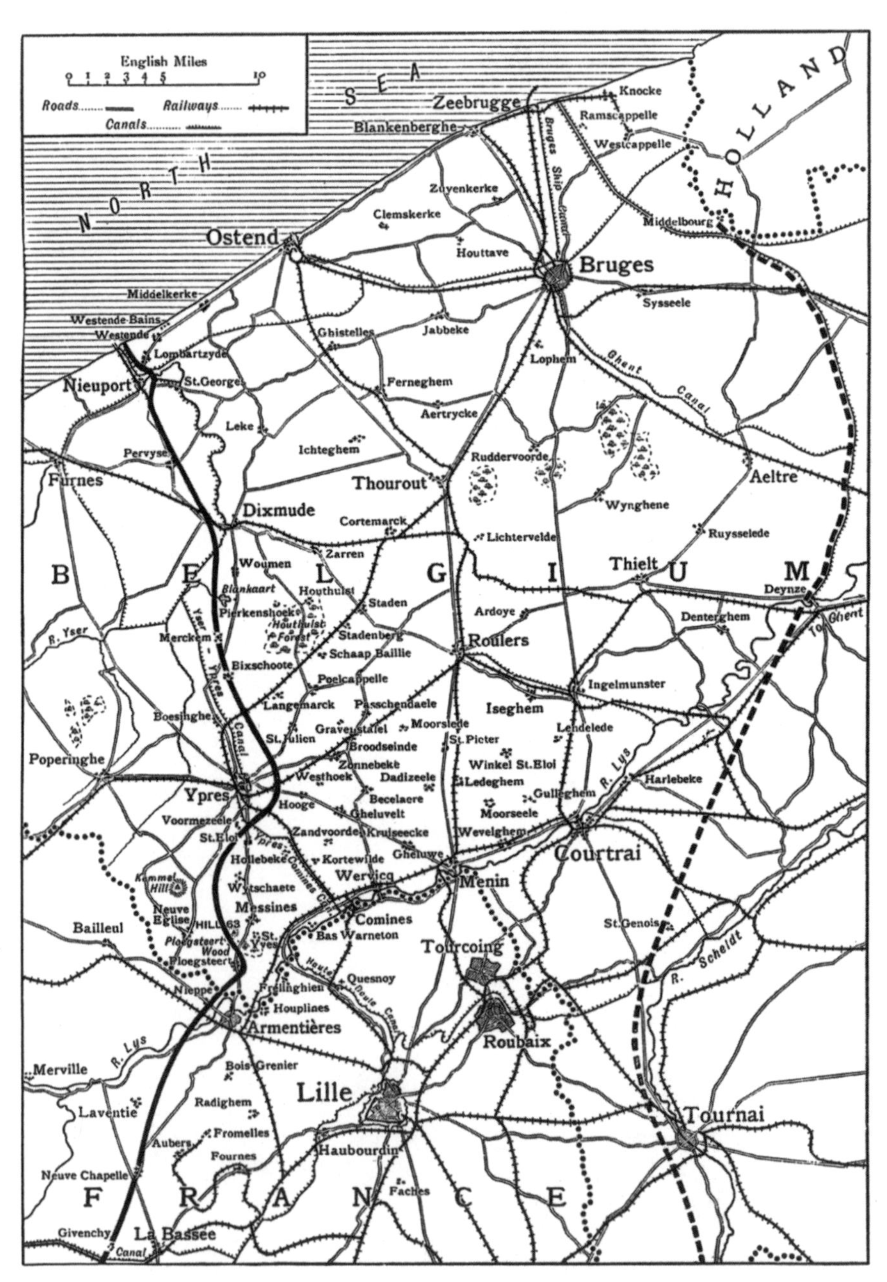

The Final Advance in Flanders, September - November, 1918.

Historical Overview
The Final Advance in Flanders, September -October 1918

The Royal Newfoundland Regiment in 1918

In December 1917 the Newfoundland Regiment received its unique honour of becoming The "Royal" Newfoundland Regiment. This was a very special compliment, but could have done little to satisfy the many grieving families back home. Over the next few months The Regiment spent a quiet period near Ypres. There they spent time on working parties, an occasional tour in the front line and resting. However a dark shadow was looming across the Western front. Everyone knew the Germans were about to launch their greatest offensive of the war. The question was only where and when.

On March 21st, 1918 the first blow was struck on the Somme. In savage fighting the German army advanced 80 km and came close to capturing the vital city of Amiens. By April 5th the German advance on the Somme, stymied by the courageous defence of British, French, Australian, New Zealander and South African troops, was fought to a standstill.

In April the Huns launched another major offensive astride the Lys river, south of Ypres. In this action the 29th Division, including The Royal Newfoundland Regiment, were thrown into battle in a desperate attempt to stop the Germans. On April 12th-14th, 1918 in the Battle of Bailleul the Newfoundlanders counter-attacked German positions near Steenwerck. They successfully held their gains for two days until ordered to make a fighting retreat. The cost had been 176 killed and wounded.

The Regiment was withdrawn from the line in late April, and short of reinforcements and under strength, was removed from the 29th Division. They were no longer to be in the fighting, instead they were to be used as Lines of Communications troops. This was a shock to the men. They were proud to be part of the "incomparable" 29th Division. It had been an honour for them to serve alongside such famous Regiments and with such a courageous group of men.

The Royal Newfoundland Regiment remained behind the lines until the Final Advance to Victory started. In September 1918 they once again became a fighting unit, and were sent to the 28th Infantry Brigade of the 9th (Scottish) Division. They were to be part of the final advance in Flanders.

The Final Advance in Flanders, September 28th-November 11th, 1918

The German Offensives in the spring of 1918 had inflicted massive losses on the Allies, captured hundreds of miles of territory but failed in its main objective of breaking the French and British Armies.

In mid-July the Allies struck back at Compiegne. On August 8th, 1918 a combined Canadian-Australian-British-French force smashed the Germans in front of Amiens and drove them back almost 15 km. It was known as the "catastrophe of 8th of August" or "the Black Day of the German Army". The tide of war had turned.

The Allied plan was to keep striking at the enemy, applying continuous pressure all along the Western Front. It was to be one hammer blow after another. Through August and into September the Allied armies hammered at the German lines, constantly driving them back.

One of the fronts chosen for attack at the end of September was the Ypres Salient. This tiny toe of Belgium, the only unoccupied piece of Belgian territory, had been the scene of some of the most brutal battles of the Great War. For four years it had been a front-line Hell, costing the lives of 250,000 British Empire soldiers. Now on September 28th, 1918 it was to see its final battle. The great breakthrough at Ypres was about to take place. King Albert of Belgium had the honour of commanding this important stroke. Included in his force was the 9th (Scottish) Division, and one of its newly assigned battalions of infantry was the 1st Battalion, The Royal Newfoundland Regiment.

The Battle of Ypres, September 28th-October 2nd, 1918

The plan for the attack on September 28th, 1918 was to hit the Germans, already stretched thin along a 24 km front. The role of the 9th Division was to break through the German positions along the infamous Menin Road. At 5:30 a.m. the men of the 9th Division cut through the enemy lines. The Newfoundlanders, now mostly inexperienced troops, followed-up the advance. They captured Polygon Wood, a death trap in 1917, with only 15 casualties. By the day's end they had advanced 8 km.

They were now facing the German's Flanders I Stellung defensive line, running north-south along the undulating landscape south of Roulers (Roselare) to Menin (Menen).

The attack commenced the next day. At 9 a.m., without an artillery barrage, the Regiment moved over the crest of the Keiberg Ridge. At once the enemy machine-guns and artillery opened fire and the first Newfoundlanders fell. Undeterred, in small groups they advanced, farm by farm, and took many prisoners. The men had a couple of problems in that they did not have artillery support and the Germans were using every farm house as a defensive position. Casualties were mounting, but the persistence of the attackers was paying off. By 4 p.m. they had reached the Roulers-Menin road. (Since the First World War many place names have reverted to earlier Flemish titles. Today it is the Roeselare-Menen road.) In two days of fighting the Newfoundlanders had advanced 14 km at a cost of only 100 killed and wounded. Sadly amongst the fallen was Lieutenant Herbert Rendell. His brother, Cliff had been mortally wounded at Beaumont-Hamel in July 1916 and died three weeks later. Lieutenant Lionel Duley of the Royal Newfoundland Regiment's hockey team was also killed September 29th, 1918.

The Push continued into October. On the 2nd the Newfoundlanders captured Ledeghem (now Ledegem) Station in the face of Machine-gun and sniper fire. It was now "open warfare" and the men of the Royal Newfoundland Regiment, through individual acts of bravery and ingenuity, were adapting quickly.

The Battle of Courtrai, October 14th-19th, 1918

All along the Western Front the Allies struck the Germans positions and kept up constant pressure. The Flanders attack was to be renewed on October 14th, 1918. They had waited a week for the artillery to come forward and to give the attacking Divisions a rest. This time the 9th (Scottish) Division, including the Royal Newfoundland Regiment, faced a difficult, if less established, German position. Once again the Germans would utilize every possible geographic feature and every farm house to thwart the attackers.

At 5:35 a.m. behind a barrage and a heavy ground mist the Newfoundlanders left their positions north of Ledeghem and moved eastward. The mist enabled the attackers to close with the enemy, but as it cleared the Germans opened up with machine-guns and the battle devolved to small group actions. The men, in twos and threes, would outflank a German position. Many prisoners were taken.

Quite quickly the hamlet of Neerhof was captured. The advance was now slowed by an open field, one km across and cut diagonally by a stream called the Wulfdambeek. The Germans had complete domination over the battlefield from a ridge and as the Newfoundlanders started to cross they were cut down. The main German resistance came from a farm on top of a small ridge. With no artillery to assist them, a small band of men made their way south of the ridge. There they could see German guns firing from another small hamlet, Drie-Masten. They closed to within 300 metres of the guns and engaged them with their Lewis guns, until their ammunition ran out. A 17 year-old Private, Thomas Ricketts volunteered to go back and get some more ammunition. Ricketts crossed 100 metres under heavy fire, grabbed the new supplies and once again crossed the bullet-swept fields returning to the gun position. The men of the Royal Newfoundland Regiment, re-armed, quickly forced the Germans to withdraw, and then pounced on the retiring enemy capturing four artillery pieces, four machine-guns and 8 prisoners.

The advance continued for another one km before stalling in front of Laaga Kapel Wood. It had been a great day. They had advanced 5 km, but lost 26 men killed or mortally wounded. Private Thomas Ricketts of Middle Arm, Newfoundland was later awarded the Victoria Cross for his bravery on October 14th, 1918. His was the only V.C. given to the Newfoundlanders during the First World War.

On October 15th the men renewed their advance. Now they were encountering many refugees as well as an assortment of Germans surrendering. It seemed the end of the war was in sight.

On October 20th the Royal Newfoundland Regiment participated in an action to cross the Lys canal at Harlebeke. All bridges had been destroyed so they used pontoon bridges and rafts for crossing. Elements of three British Divisions made the attack and within two hours, in the face of enemy resistance, they were across. At 4 a.m. the Newfoundlanders paddled over the Lys to support the attack. In the afternoon they liberated Deerlyck (now Deerlijk), and led the attack on Vichte. German opposition had stiffened considerably and the Newfoundlanders were finally stopped on the western outskirts of the village. By this time the battalion strength of the Royal

Newfoundlanders was a mere 256 men, a quarter of a full battalion's complement.

Action of Ooteghem, October 25th, 1918

The Newfoundland Battalion's final action of the Great War took place near Ingoyhen (now Ingooigem) in what became officially known as the Action of Ooteghem (now Otegem). It was to be a continuation of the earlier fighting, and the objective was the Ooteghem-Ingoyghem Ridge, one of the last barriers in front of the Scheldt canal. The position was strongly defended and when the men started the assault at 9 a.m., it became very obvious that any advance would cost a lot of lives. By the afternoon the Newfoundlanders had captured Ingoyghem, but their move towards Ooteghem met heavy fire. Given that the resistance had stiffened and that the end of the war was known to be near, the advance was called off. On October 26th, 1918 the 1st Battalion, The Royal Newfoundland Regiment was withdrawn from the fighting for the last time in the war. Their last action had cost 19 lives.

The Battalion was at Cuerne (now Kuurne) when the war ended. The Final advance in Flanders had cost the Newfoundlanders 429 casualties, including 90 dead. The long road which had started at Suvla Bay in September 1915, had ended more than three years later not far from Courtrai (now Kortrijk), Belgium. It had been a difficult and costly experience that deeply scarred the people of the Empire's oldest colony.

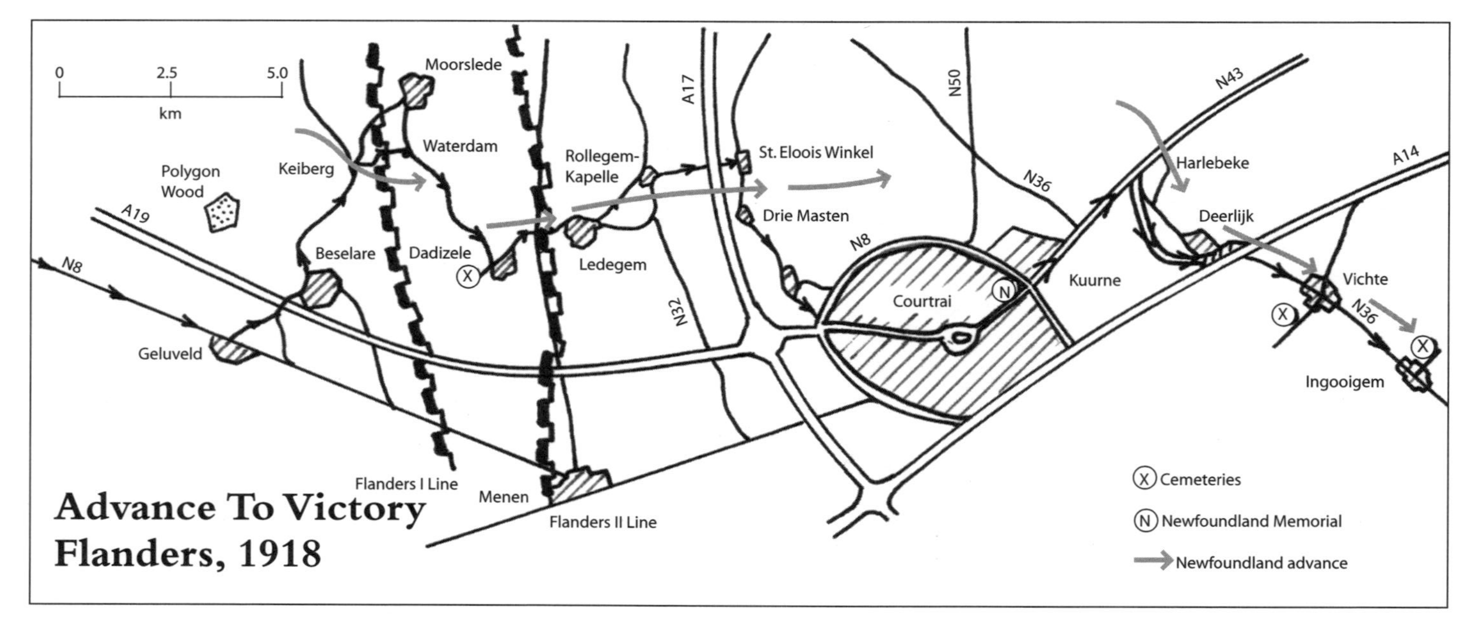

Tour map: The Advance of the Royal Newfoundland Regiment, September - October, 1918.

The Tour- Courtrai, 1918

The tour of the Final Advance in Flanders is a challenging one. It covers 40 km, through relatively busy areas. It is recommended you review your maps (use the IGN maps 28/3-4 and 29/1-2) and have a navigator with whom you have a healthy relationship. Don't be afraid of U-turns.

The tour starts in the Grote Markt of Ypres (now Ieper). Exit via the Menen road (N6) and follow the N8 to Geluveld (formerly Gheluvelt). You are driving through the most infamous British Empire battlefield of the First World War. For the attack of September 28th, 1918 the Newfoundlanders advanced north of the N8, following the successful assault of the 9th Division. At Geluveld take the small road on the left taking you over the A19 to Beselare (formerly Becelare) three km away. Go through Beselare following the N303 and just outside the village take a small road leading north-west to Keiberg. You will reach Keiberg after 4 km. The ridge north of the hamlet was where the Newfoundlanders advanced on September 29th. As they crossed the low ground near Keiberg they were swept by machine-gun fire and suffered 15 killed. The Flanders I line ran north-south over the Keiberg Ridge. Prior to this attack this area was untouched by war. (However Passchendaele village is 4 km west. The area from that village west to Ypres was utter desolation after four years of battle.) The Flanders I line was mainly concrete bunkers and barbed-wire. It provided only a minor deterrent to the attackers.

Exit Keiberg heading north-east and after 400 metres take the small road on the right towards another hamlet, Waterdam. Turn right at Waterdam towards Dadizele (formerly Dadizeele), 3.5 km away. In Dadizeele turn right following the CWGC signs to Dadizeele New British Cemetery, 500 metres distant.

Dadizeele New British Cemetery contains 1,029 Commonwealth burials including 19 Newfoundlanders. The majority of the burials are soldiers killed September 28th-October 2nd, 1918, in the breaking of the Flanders I line. There is a large German bunker in the southern part of the cemetery. It was typical of the German fortifications in the area. A German position south-east of Dadizele, known as Hill 41 held up the British attack on the Flanders II line. However the 9th Division, with the Newfoundlanders in the lead, was successful in cracking the Flanders II line on October 2nd. In fact they pushed into Ledegem (formerly Ledeghem).

To follow the next phase of the advance of the Royal Newfoundland Regiment exit Dadizele on the north-east towards Ledegem. The capture of Ledegem was an exceptional achievement. On October 1st, 1918 the men left their positions north of Dadizele. Covered by an early mist they advanced north of the road you are driving on, and crossed the Roselare-Menen (N32) road. They swept the enemy before them and pierced the Flanders II position getting as far as Ledegem. Here they were halted on a north-south railway line (no longer there) that ran by the western edge of the village.

You enter the village through Kapelhoek. The railway ran parallel with the road leading through the village centre. After October 2nd there was a delay in resuming the advance due to bad roads and a disorganized supply system. The Newfoundlanders received a welcomed rest, but on October 14th, they were back at it. This time their assault would lead to their one and only Victoria Cross of the war.

To follow the advance of October 14th, 1918 exit Ledegem on the north-east towards Rollegem-Kapelle (2 km). The advance took place in the fields south of the village. In Rollegem turn right and after 400 metres you reach Neerhof. This cluster of farm buildings was captured early on the 14th. Just past Neerhof turn left on a small unnumbered road. Cutting across the field south of you is a small stream, the Wulfsdambeek. It cuts the field diagonally, and was a terrific obstacle to the attackers. The field was controlled by the Germans from the ridge one km in front of you. Today the German position is cut in half by the A17 Motorway (to Brugge). The Germans from their positions near the Motorway were inflicting heavy casualties on the Newfoundlanders. A small group moved south of the ridge, endeavouring to silence the Germans. Unfortunately this area of their advance is obscured by the Motorway.

Continue on the small road until it ends at the A17. Turn left and then right on the road going under the A17 to St. Eloois-Winkel. Once under the A17 turn right on a small road running parallel to the A17. After two km you have come to the site of Tommy Ricketts famous V.C. action.

Looking east you can see a small collection of buildings which is the

The field over which the Newfoundlanders advanced October 14th 1918. The ridge which held up the advance is mid-horizon. Ricketts won his V.C. south-east of the ridge. (N. Christie)

German bunker in Dadizeele British Cemetery (N. Christie)

hamlet of Drie-Masten. There were several German batteries operating near Drie-Masten. A small group, including Ricketts, had made their way south of the ridge (visible west of you) and started to fire at the enemy guns. They ran out of ammunition and Ricketts volunteered to cross the bullet-swept fields to get more. This he did. He ran across the terrain in front of you, collected more Lewis gun panniers and rejoined his comrades. It was amazing that he survived. With their ammunition supply replenished the band of Newfoundlanders captured the enemy batteries and continued their advance.

The 17 year-old Ricketts was awarded the Victoria Cross. His citation reads:

The attack was temporarily held up by hostile fire and the platoon to which he belonged suffered severe casualties from the fire of a battery a point blank range.

Pte. Ricketts at once volunteered to go forward with his section commander and a Lewis gun team to attempt to outflank the battery. Advancing by short rushes under heavy fire from enemy machine-guns with the hostile battery, their ammunition was exhausted when still 300 yards from the battery. The enemy, seeing an opportunity to get their field guns away, began to bring up their gun teams. Pte. Ricketts, at once realising the situation, doubled back 100 yards under the heaviest machine-gun fire, procured further ammunition, and dashed back again to the Lewis gun, and by very accurate fire drove the enemy and the gun teams into a farm.

His platoon then advanced without casualties, and captured four field guns, four machine-guns and eight prisoners.

A fifth field gun was subsequently intercepted by fire and captured.

The attack continued on October 15th, when the 9th Division and the Newfoundlanders liberated 3 km more of Belgium. Finally they halted near St. Katarina-Kapelle (formerly St. Catherine-Capelle).

The advance had cost the Newfoundlanders; 17 killed in action and 11 died of wounds. But the war was almost over. All along the Western Front the Germans were retiring and massive armies, British, French, Belgian and American, were continuously battering the foe.

For the final chapter in Newfoundland, return to St.Eloois-Winkel and take the road to Gullegem (formerly Gulleghem). You are driving over the battlefield of October 15th and will pass

The Courtrai Caribou. (N. Christie)

Sergeant Thomas Ricketts, VC.

through Drie-Masten, just before reaching Gullegem. Go through Gullegem and exit south-east towards Courtrai (or Kortijk), getting on the N8 Ring road to Harlebeke. After 6 km the road crosses the Lys River and from the bridge you can see the Newfoundland Memorial Caribou. At the lights turn right on the N43 to visit the Memorial. It is situated where the Newfoundlanders were billetted when the war ended on November 11th, 1918 and it commemorates their sacrifices in the Final Advance in Flanders. It is an out-of-place location for the majestic beast. It is a very busy street, a long way from the heavy fighting of the First World War.

Continue 4 km east on the N43 to Harlebeke. At Harlebeke take the N36 south towards Vichte. Where the N36 meets the N43 is roughly where the Newfoundlanders paddled across the Lys to join the attack on October 20th. (They actually crossed at Beveren one km north of Harlebeke.) Follow the N36 over the A14/E17 Motorway, to Vichte, the scene of fighting on the 20th, when The Regiment led the attack on the village. They were unable to secure it, but dug in on the western outskirts of Vichte. One km west of the village is Vichte Military Cemetery. It contains 236 burials, including 60 unknowns. Eleven of the graves belong to Newfoundlanders, including three unknowns.

The final action of the war takes place along the three km stretch of N36 between Vichte and Ingooigem (formerly Ingoyghem). It was part of the main assault on the Ingoyghem Ridge. The attackers met heavy fire and their attack was called off without taking the ridge. It was the last of the fighting for the 1st Battalion, The Royal Newfoundland Regiment. On the north-east side of the village of Ingooiem is the Military Cemetery. It contains 84 burials or commemorations. They are men of the 9th Division who fell in their last attack of the war. Amongst them are three Newfoundlanders; Isaac Penny of Bonavista Bay, James Power of Harbour Grace and Joseph Daley of St. John's. They died such a long, long way from Home.

To return to Ypres go back to the N43, follow it to Courtrai (Kortijk) and then rejoin the north N8 Ring Road. After 6 km take the exit for theA19 Motorway to Ypres (Ieper), 20 km away. To return to Arras (65 km) follow the N36 to the A14/E17 Motorway, get on going south to Lille and Paris. Around Lille follow the A1 Motorway to Paris and get off at the Arras exit. (These routes can be used in reverse for the quickest visit to the Newfoundland Memorial Park at Courtrai.)

Cemeteries and Memorials

The Beaumont-Hamel Memorial

One of the founding principles of the Imperial (Commonwealth) War Graves Commission was that the name of every soldier, sailor or airman who died in the war would be remembered either on a headstone in a cemetery, or if the grave was unknown or lost, by name on a Memorial to the Missing.

After the First World War Newfoundland made the unique decision to commemorate all its missing, whether Navy, Merchant Marine or Army, all on one Memorial. The chosen location of the Memorial was at Beaumont-Hamel, where the Newfoundlanders had made their greatest sacrifice of the war.*

The Memorial is arrayed in three bronze panels at the base of the Caribou, and it reads:

TO THE GLORY OF GOD AND IN PERPETUAL REMEMBRANCE OF THOSE OFFICERS AND MEN OF THE NEWFOUNDLAND FORCES WHO GAVE THEIR LIVES BY LAND AND SEA IN THE GREAT WAR AND HAVE NO KNOWN GRAVE.
"LET THEM GIVE GLORY UNTO THE LORD AND DECLARE HIS PRAISE IN THE ISLANDS." ISAIAH 42-12.

It records the names of 820 Newfoundlanders who have no known grave. Of the names of the Missing:

-114 belonged to the Newfoundland Royal Naval Reserve who died serving with the Royal Navy,

-115 were lost with the Mercantile Marine, and

-591 belonged to the Royal Newfoundland Regiment.

** There is one exception; Second Lieutenant Harold G. Barrett, killed in action on August 16th, 1917 is commemorated on Panel 161 of the Tyne Cot Memorial to the Missing. I have been unable to determine the reason for this unusual place of commemoration. It appears to have been an oversight.*

The men of the Regiment listed here include those who lost their lives in Gallipoli and on the Western Front and "to whom the fortune of war denied the known and honoured burial given to their comrades in death." This means half of those killed fighting on the Western Front are missing and have no known grave.

The majority of those missing are from the fighting on July 1st, 1916 (131 names), at Monchy on April 14th, 1917 (140 names) and at Masnieres, November 20th- December 3rd,1917 (54 names).

The graves of five Newfoundlanders were found after the Memorial was erected in 1925. These men are buried in Serre Road No. 2 and London Cemetery and Extension.

The Memorials are always less personal than the cemeteries and something is lost reading a long list of names. But the Newfoundland Memorial is so small by CWGC standards that by reviewing the names on the bronze panels you are struck by the repetition of surnames. The same family name appears again and again and knowing these men were native Newfoundlanders, from small compact communities, one can only speculate about the cost to the towns and outports across the Island.

There are 17 sets of brothers named on the Memorial, and many others whose sibling lies buried nearby. Three quarters of those remembered here were only 21 years old or younger when they lost their lives in battle. Private William Morgan was only 16 when he was killed at Beaumont-Hamel.

Brothers Fred and George Abbott of St. John's were killed July 1st, 1916 and are commemorated here, as are Hector and William Bennett, killed at Monchy, April 14th, 1917.

Amongst those listed is Second Lieutenant Gerald W. Ayre, son of Frederick and Mary Julia Ayre of St. John's. He was 25 when he was killed at Beaumont-Hamel. His brother, Captain Bernard Pitts Ayre was also killed July 1st, while serving with the 8th Battalion, The Norfolk Regiment. He is buried in Carnoy Military Cemetery (south-east of Albert, Row D, Grave 10. Their cousin, Captain Eric Ayre, 1st Battalion, The Newfoundland Regiment, son of Robert and Lydia Ayre of St. John's, killed July 1st, is buried in Ancre British Cemetery, II.E.12. Another cousin, Second Lieutenant Wilfred D. Ayre, age 21, was also killed July 1st with the Newfoundlanders. He was the son of Charles and Diana Ayre, also of St. John's. He is buried in Knightsbridge Cemetery, B.10.

Statistics - Newfoundland in the Great War

Newfoundland - Total Population (1911) - 242,619
-Total Male Population (1911) - 124,305

Royal Newfoundland Regiment
Enlistments
-Royal Newfoundland Regiment - 6,326
Served - Overseas - 5,046
- France and Belgium - 4,253
- Gallipoli - 1,178

Casualties
-Killed in action - 846 (18 Gallipoli)
-Died of wounds - 253 (13 Gallipoli)
-Died, other causes - 102 (18 Gallipoli)
Total dead - 1,201
-wounded - 2,314 (93 Gallipoli)
-prisoners - 150

Other Newfoundland Enlistments
Newfoundland Forestry Corps Enlistments - 481
-casualties - 3 dead(accidentally)
Newfoundland Royal Naval Reserve - 2,053
-casualties - 167 killed in action
Newfoundland Mercantile Marine - estimated 1,500
-casualties - 155 lost at sea (enemy action)
Nurses - 43
Canadian and other forces - 3,200

-During the war 11,879 or 9.5% of Newfoundland men served.
-Of the 4,253 soldiers of the Royal Newfoundland Regiment who served in France and Belgium, 1,152 died. The fatality rate of 27% was the highest of any combatants on the Western Front.
-Total deaths, all branches, resulting from war service total 1,526 or 1.22% of the entire male population of Newfoundland.

The names of three of the men who saved Monchy in April 1917 are listed on the panels: Sergeant Joseph Waterfield, MM was killed at Ypres, Ocober 9th, 1917; Sergeant Walter Pitcher, MM was killed at Masnieres, November 20th, 1917 and Lance Corporal Japheth Hounsell, MM was killed at the Lys, April 13th, 1918. Amongst the many other names is the "Eskimo" sniper, John Shiwak of Rigolet, Labrador. He was killed and buried at Masnieres during the Battle of Cambrai and his grave was later lost.

The British soldiers who died fighting shoulder-to-shoulder with the Newfoundlanders are commemorated on several Memorials to the Missing: Thiepval (The Battle of the Somme, 72,000 names), Arras Memorial at Faubourg D'Amiens (The Battle of Arras, 35,696 names), The Cambrai Memorial, Louerval (The Battle of Cambrai, 7,000 names), the Tyne Cot Memorial (The Final Advance in Flanders, 1918, 35,000 names) and The Helles Memorial, Gallipoli (21,000 names).

Beaumont-Hamel Memorial, 1928. (PANF)

The graves of the men of Newfoundland are scattered in war cemeteries from Gallipoli, to St. John's. There are small numbers buried in Egypt, on the island of Limnos in the Aegean, and in Germany (for those who died as prisoners). There is even a Newfoundlander buried in Switzerland. But the vast majority rest in military cemeteries in France and Belgium. They are buried amongst the seas of headstones that mark the sacrifice of the British Empire. They stand out by their unique national symbol, the caribou, carved into each of their headstones.

Beaumont-Hamel, July 1st, 1916

Of the 271 Newfoundlanders who were killed on July 1st, 1916 or died as a result of wounds received that day, half have no known grave and are commemorated on the Beaumont-Hamel Memorial. More than 100 who have a known grave are buried in the cemeteries in or near the Park. The cemeteries were made by the V Army Corps in the winter of 1917. V Corps was given the responsibility of clearing the old Somme battlefield after the Germans had withdrawn to the Hindenburg line. Many of the corpses interred in the 20 cemeteries made by V Corps in the area had lain out in No Man's Land since July 1st, 1916. Needless to say, the task of identifying and burying the largely skeletal remains was a gruesome one.

Y Ravine Cemetery, Beaumont-Hamel Memorial Park

Y Ravine Cemetery contains the graves or commemorations of 428 Commonwealth soldiers (153 are unidentified). Forty-five of the burials are Newfoundlanders (9 are unidentified). One of those graves is that of Lieutenant Hubert Herder, aged 25, of St. John's. He was one of a few surviving officers that had tried to rally the men at the Danger Tree. Herder was killed shortly after. His brother, Second Lieutenant Arthur J. Herder died on December 1st, 1917, of wounds received near Marcoing Wood. He is buried in Tincourt New British Cemetery. They were the sons of William and Elizabeth Herder of St. John's.

Private John J. Carew is buried in D.111. His brother, David, was killed at Gallipoli, October 7th, 1915. They were the sons of David and Carrie Carew of St. John's.

Buried in Row D, Grave 21 is Private Francis Thomas Lind. Lind's letters home had been published in the newspapers in 1915-1916 and

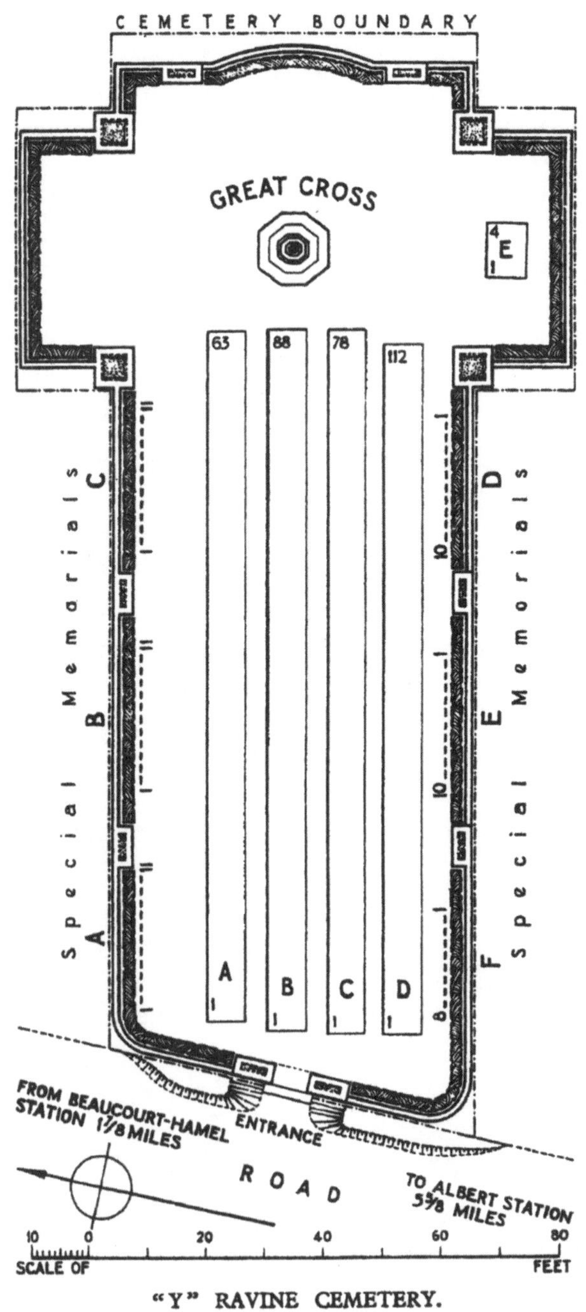

"Y" RAVINE CEMETERY.

Lieutenant Hubert C. Herder
St. John's, Age 25.
Killed in action July 1st, 1916.
Buried Y Ravine Cemetery, C.69.
(His brother, Arthur, died of wounds
December 1st, 1917.)

Sergeant Edward F, Gladney
Placentia Bay. Age 22.
Killed in action July 1st, 1916.
Buried Y Ravine Cemetery, D.19.

Private Charles F. Taylor
St. John's. Age 23.
Killed in action July 1st, 1916.
Buried Y Ravine Cemetery, C.3.

Lieutenant Richard A, Shortall
St. John's.
Killed in action July 1st, 1916.
Buried Y Ravine Cemetery, C.44.

had provided the folks at home with an often humourous insight into life overseas. Known as "Mayo" Lind, because he was always asking for cigarettes, he became an unofficial and popular spokesman for the "Boys". He was 37 years old when he was killed on July 1st, 1916. In 1919 a collection of his letters were published as "Letters of Mayo Lind". (The book was republished in 2001 by Creative Publishing, St. John's.)

Most of the identified burials in the cemetery belong to men of the Gordon Highlanders, killed November 13th, 1916, the 1st Battalion, Royal Inniskilling Fusiliers and the 2nd South Wales Borderers killed July 1st, 1916.

There was a second Y Ravine Cemetery adjacent to the current site but it was removed after the war to Ancre British Cemetery.

The second cemetery in the Park, Hunter's Cemetery, contains 46 men of the 51st Highland Division, killed November 13th, 1916. The men were buried in a large shell crater. It is a mass grave.

Hawthorne Ridge Cemetery, No.2, Beaumont-Hamel Memorial Park

This cemetery contains 214 Commonwealth graves including 24 Newfoundlanders (8 are unidentified). The graves belong to men of the 29th Division killed July 1st, 1916. The majority of the graves belong to soldiers of the 2nd Battalion Royal Fusiliers and the 1st Battalion, The Border Regiment. Amongst the Newfoundlanders buried here is Sergeant Thomas Carroll of Harbour Grace. Carroll was rumoured to be the only man who made it into the German trenches on July 1st, but based on where he is buried this is unlikely. He was 46 years old, one of the oldest men from Newfoundland to die in the war. Sergeant Carroll is buried in Row A, Grave 40.

Sergeant F. Lloyd, 2nd Battalion, The South Wales Borderers, is buried in A.65. In 1992 it was discovered that he had a second apparent grave in Miraumont Communal Cemetery, A.8. This cemetery was used exclusively by the Germans for the burial of prisoners. Examination of the original records indicated that a "Lloyds, South Wales Borderers" had been buried there with two other men of the Regiment, but the Germans had indicated a date of death of April 30th, 1916. Examination of the SWB Roll of Honour showed three men missing in a raid on April 29th, 1916, including a Private H. Lloyd. Matching the date of death

Lieutenant Frederick C. Mellor
Annapolis Royal, Nova Scotia. Age 28.
Killed in action July 1st, 1916.
Buried Knightsbridge Cemetery, B.9.

Private Robert J. Lahey
Bell Island. Age 28.
Killed in action July 1st, 1916.
Buried Knightsbridge Cemetery, H.2.

Sergeant Thomas Carroll
Harbour Grace. Age 46.
Killed in action July 1st, 1916.
Buried Hawthorn Ridge No. 2 Cemetery, A.40.

Lance Corporal Arthur J. Rendell
St. John's. Age 20.
Killed in action July 1st, 1916.
Buried Hawthorn Ridge No. 2 Cemetery, A.15.

Ancre British Cemetery, circa 1922.

Y Ravine Cemetery, circa 1925.

allowed for an identification of the grave of Private Lloyd and his two missing comrades. The appropriate headstones were erected over the graves in 1993.

From the northern side of the cemetery, Hawthorn Ridge No. 1 Cemetery (containing 153 graves, including one Newfoundlander) and the trees growing out of Hawthorn Crater can be scene.

Knightsbridge Cemetery, Mesnil-Martinsart

Knightbridge Cemetery is located in an open field 1.5 km south-east of Auchonvillers. Access is via the D174 to Mesnil-Martinsart and down a 600 metre dirt road. Due to the possibility of getting stuck, it is recommended to walk in from the D174. It was named after a Communication Trench that ran to the front lines in the Park 500 metres distant.

It contains the graves of 584 soldiers, including 39 Newfoundlanders (16 are unidentified). The cemetery was used throughout the war and it was enlarged after the armistice when an additional 190 graves were brought in from the surrounding battlefields. Most of the Newfoundlanders buried here (Rows G and H) were exhumed from their original graves inside the Park after the war.

Amongst the original burials in the cemetery is Second Lieutenant Wilfred Ayre (B.10), one of the four Ayre family members killed on July 1st. He was one of Gerald and Bernard Ayre's two cousins.

Ancre British Cemetery, Beaumont-Hamel

Ancre British Cemetery is located on the D50 to Beaucourt, 200 metres north of the village of Hamel. It is 1.5 km south-east of The Park. It was an original V Corps cemetery that was greatly enlarged by battlefield clearances after the war. Its burials reflect the terrific fighting that took place between Beaumont-Hamel and the Ancre river in the summer and fall of 1916. It now contains 2,540 Commonwealth graves of which 1,335 are unidentified. There are 32 Newfoundlanders buried in Ancre British Cemetery, including 8 unknowns.

Amongst the burials is Captain Eric Ayre, (II. E.12.) the cousin of brothers Gerald and Bernard Ayre, of St. John's. The Newfoundlanders buried here were originally buried in Y Ravine Cemetery No. 2. After the war they were concentrated to Ancre.

The burials in Ancre British Cemetery are predominantly men of the

63 rd Royal Naval Division killed November 13th, 1916 and men of the 36th (Ulster) and 29th Divisions killed July 1st, 1916. The Newfoundlanders are predominantly buried in Plots II and VI.

The afore-mentioned cemeteries hold the largest numbers of men of The Newfoundland Regiment killed July 1st, 1916. There are numerous other cemeteries that contain smaller numbers of Newfoundlanders who died in this battle. (Please consult the Michelin (Commonwealth War Graves Overprint) Maps numbers 51, 52 and 53 for their locations.) They are: Auchonvillers Military Cemetery (8), Beaumont-Hamel British Cemetery (1), Beauval Communal Cemetery (5 died of wounds), Gezaincourt Communal Cemetery Extension (6 died of wounds), Doullens Communal Cemetery Extension No. 1 (4 died of wounds).

Due to the incredible number of remains resurfacing through the 1920s and 1930s several cemeteries were left open or reopened for burials. For example between 1921 and 1925, 20,000 remains were found, even in 1934, 738 bodies were recovered from the Somme battlefield. Two of these cemeteries in particular involved the discovery of Newfoundlanders.

Serre Road Cemetery No.2, Beaumont-Hamel

The cemetery is located on the road from Arras to Amiens (D919), south of the hamlet of Serre. It was the scene of fierce fighting in the summer and fall of 1916. Initially it was a V Corps battlefield cemetery, but between 1922 and 1934 7,000 remains were buried here (French farmers were paid 10 francs per body). The cemetery now contains 7,139 Commonwealth graves, including 28 Newfoundlanders.

During the winter of 1929-30 rain uncovered the remains of 26 Newfoundlanders. They were all found between the entrance of Beaumont-Hamel Park and the Caribou Memorial. These were men killed in the early part of the advance, before the British front line was reached. Four of the remains were identified, the others remain unknown to this day. Twenty-five of the Newfoundlanders are buried in Plots XXIX and XXX.

The four known burials are dually commemorated. As they were missing when the original bronze panels for the Beaumont-Hamel Memorial were cast, their names are still on the Memorial.

London Cemetery & Extension, High Wood

The cemetery is located on the D107 between Martinpuich and Longueval. Originally it was a small cemetery containing the graves of London men killed at High Wood. In the 1930s it was reopened and since then it has received more than 3,500 remains. London Cemetery & Extension is still receiving burials.

In the winter of 1936 the skeletons of 4 Newfoundland soldiers were found in an old shell hole near the entrance to Beaumont-Hamel Park. One was identified by his ID disk, as being Private M.J. Cahill, who was killed on July 1st, 1916. The other three could not be identified. Private Cahill, the last identified Newfoundlander to be found, is buried in Plot VI, Row C, Grave 26.

Gueudecourt, October 12th, 1916

Of the 76 Newfoundlanders who lost their lives at Gueudecourt in October 1916, 42 or 55% are commemorated by name only on the Beaumont-Hamel Memorial. Of those who received a known burial 17 died of wounds and rest in a Hospital Centre cemetery and of the balance 11 rest in Bancourt British Cemetery.

This is typical of the First World War battles such as The Somme, such fierce fighting, back and forth over the same ground meant only a small percentage of men killed in action have a known grave. Firstly, no lives would be risked to bury the dead. Secondly, in 1916 there was not the organization in place to bury and register the graves; consequently many were lost or destroyed in later battles. The poor treatment the dead received on the Somme demoralized the survivors and this contributed to the origins of the Directorate of Graves Registration and Enquiries. Thirdly, the British Army had yet to go to the dual identification tag system. Most soldiers carried an aluminium bracelet or ID tag worn around their neck however, this was often removed from the body so when it came time to re-inter there was no means of identification.

Bancourt British Cemetery, Bapaume

Bancourt is a small village three km east of Bapaume just south of the N30 to Cambrai. Bancourt British Cemetery is at the eastern edge of the village. It is 6 km north-east of Gueudecourt. It contains the graves of 2,480 Commonwealth soldiers, including 13 Newfoundlanders (two are unidentified).

The burials reflect fighting over an extensive period, but the graves belong predominantly to those killed in the later stages of the Battle of the Somme, the German Offensive of March-April 1918 and the Advance to Victory, August-September 1918.

Amongst the Newfoundlanders buried here is Private Oswald Goodyear (VIII.M.5.) of Grand Falls. He is one of 6 Goodyears who served in the war and one of three that were killed. His brother Lieutenant Stanley Goodyear, MC, was killed near Langemarck in October 1917 and is commemorated on the Beaumont-Hamel Memorial. Lieutenant Hedley Goodyear served with the Canadians and was sniped August 22nd, 1918. He is buried in Hillside Cemetery on the Amiens battlefield. The story of the Goodyear family is recorded in *The Danger Tree* by David Macfarlane (1991).

Heilly Station Cemetery, Mericourt-L'Abbe

Heilly-Station Cemetery is three km south of the village of Mericourt-L'Abbe, which is 8 km south-west of Albert. It was used for treatment of the wounded by Casualty Clearing Stations in 1916-1917. It now contains 2,890 Commonwealth graves (and 83 Germans) iclud-ing 2,354 British, 402 Australians, 118 New Zealanders, 6 Canadians, 1 from the Bermuda Volunteer Rifle Corps, 1 from the British West Indies Regiment and 8 Newfoundlanders. Only 12 of the 2,890 graves are unidentified.

It is located on the heights overlooking the Ancre River valley. Like many hospital centre cemeteries there is more than one man to a grave and the graves are so close together that three men are commemorated on each headstone. As there was no room for a cap badge to be engraved on each headstone, the cap badges of every unit of a man buried here are engraved on the cemeteries' entrance building.

Monchy, April 14th, 1917

The fighting at Monchy on April 14th, 1917 was the second worst day of the entire war for the Newfoundlanders. In all they lost 189 dead including those killed in action, died of wounds or taken prisoner and later died. The graves of 140 (74%) were never found or never identi-fied and are commemorated by name only on the Beaumont-Hamel

Memorial. This is typical of the later stages of the Battle of Arras when British forces unsuccessfully attacked the same German positions for a month. After the war the Labour Companies that cleared the battlefields of the dead found thousands of bodies they could not identify. The remains were interred in a number of the surrounding Military cemeteries as Unknowns. The graves of 33 Newfoundlanders were found during the clearances however only 10 could be identified.

Vis-en-Artois British Cemetery, Haucourt

The cemetery is located just east of the village of Haucourt on the D939, 12 km from Arras.

The cemetery was originally made by the Canadian Corps after a successful attack in September 1918 and was greatly enlarged after the war by the concentration of 1,901 graves from the surrounding battlefields. It now contains 2,335 Commonwealth burials including 9 from Newfoundland (6 are unidentified).

Amongst the Newfoundlanders is buried an officer killed April 14th, 1917 who could not be identified.

Dury Crucifix Cemetery, Dury

The cemetery is located on the south side of the village near the Water Tower. Dury is 3 km north of the Arras-Cambrai road (D939), 14 km from Arras.

It was started by the Canadian Corps after the breaching of the Drocourt-Queant line in September 1918. After the war the cemetery was greatly enlarged by the battlefield clearances and it now contains 2,058 Commonwealth burials, 86% are unidentified. Eleven of the graves are Newfoundlanders; 9 are unknowns.

The graves of other Newfoundlanders killed at Monchy are scattered in a number of cemeteries in the area. They are: Tilloy British Cemetery (4 unknowns), Cagnicourt British Cemetery (1 known and 3 unknowns), London Cemetery, Neuville Vitasse (3 graves) Windmill British (4 graves), and Duisans British Cemetery (12 died of wounds).

The majority of those who died as prisoners are buried in Germany (or Poland today), but some are buried in France. They are found in Tournai Communal Cemetery Allied Extension (4 burials), and Douai Communal Cemetery (5 burials).

Masnieres, November 20th-December 5th, 1917

The Battle of Cambrai cost The Newfoundland Regiment 110 dead. Of those killed 58 died in the successful advance in November and 52 died in the German counter-offensive. Of the fallen, 54 are commemorated on the Beaumont-Hamel Memorial.

Marcoing British Cemetery

The cemetery is located 2 km east of Marcoing on the south side of the road to Masnieres. It was made after the armistice by the concentration of small cemeteries in the area. It contains 372 Commonwealth burials including 24 Newfoundlanders.

The Newfoundlanders are all identified and are buried in Plot II Rows E and G. The burials here are those killed November 20th, 1917 and were originally buried by Father Nangle after the initial assault across the canal.

Rocquigny-Equancourt Road British Cemetery, Manancourt

The cemetery is located in open country on the D172, west of the crossroads with the D43, opposite the village of Etricourt. Etricourt is 12 km south-east of Bapaume. (The cemetery is 8 km south-east of Bancourt British Cemetery.)

It was made by Casualty Clearing Stations in 1917-1918. The cemetery contains 1,838 Commonwealth burials including 22 Newfoundlanders (all are identified)

Amongst the burials is that of Sergeant John Rhodes, VC, DCM, of the 3rd Battalion, Grenadier Guards, III.E.1. Rhodes won his Victoria Cross for bravery in October 1917. He died of wounds received in the Battle of Cambrai.

There are 12 Canadians buried in the cemetery. Most are men of the Canadian Cavalry Brigade who died in the Battle of Cambrai. Amongst the dozen is Private Lord Edward Beauchamp Seymour of the Lord Strathcona's Horse, who died of wounds December 5th, 1917. Age 38. He was the son of the 6th Marquess of Hertford. Lord Seymour is buried in VI.B.11.

A small number of the Newfoundland Regiment are buried in a few other cemeteries in the region. They are: Flesquieres Hill British (2 known), Gouzeaucourt New British (2 known). Villers Plouich Communal (1 known), and Tincourt New British (2 known).

Courtrai, September 28th-October 26th, 1918

The Advance to Victory in Flanders was a completely successful operation for the British forces. However it still took a toll on the attackers. The Newfoundlanders lost 93 dead from September 29th to October 25th, 1918. Of the fallen 68 have known graves and 25 are commemorated by name only on the Beaumont-Hamel Memorial. This number of “missing” (27%) is very high for such a successful attack. Perhaps with a serious review of CWGC documents some of the unknown graves could be identified.

Many of the below-mentioned cemeteries also contain Newfoundland graves from 1917 when The Regiment fought in the Third Battle of Ypres. All the cemeteries are in Belgium. Michelin Map No.51, (CWGC Overprint) should be used to help locate these cemeteries.

Tyne Cot British Cemetery, Passchendaele

Tyne Cot British Cemetery is the largest Commonwealth war cemetery in the world. It was originally started by fighting units in October 1917 and enlarged by the concentration of more than 10,000 remains recovered from the surrounding battlefields. More than 70% of the burials are unidentified. The majority of the graves are from the Third Battle of Ypres, 1917, but men killed as early as October 1914 and many killed in the Final Advance in Flanders, 1918, are also buried here.

The cemetery contains 11,871 Commonwealth burials including 14 Newfoundlanders (7 are unidentified). These men were all killed on the Keiberg Ridge September 29th, 1918. Lieutenant Lionel Duley of St. John’s and a member of the Royal Newfoundland Regimental hockey team, is buried in Plot LIII. Row H. Grave 8 (beside the German bunker on the west side of the cemetery). He was 20 years old.

The cemetery contains the graves of three Victoria Cross winners: Private J.P. Robertson, VC, 27th Battalion Canadian Infantry (LVIII.D.26.), Captain C.S. Jeffries, VC, 34th Battalion Australian Infantry (XL.E.1.) And Sergeant Lewis McGee, VC, 40th Battalion Australian Infantry (XX.D.1.).

At the rear of the cemetery a long curved wall commemorates 34,000 British soldiers and 1,150 New Zealanders killed in the Ypres Salient and who have no known graves. It is literally Part II of the listing of “Missing” that starts with the 55,000 names on the Menin Gate

An amazing photograph of the Newfoundland Regiment's Ice Hockey team with officials and spare men, circa 1917. Back row (left to right): Rex Williams, Sydney Bennett, Jack Strang, Duke Winter. Second row: Hayward Williams, Charlie Strang (killed April 13th, 1918; buried Lijssenthoek Military Cemetery, Belgium), Lionel Duley (killed September 29th, 1918; buried Tyne Cot British Cemetery, Belgium), Stan Newman. Front row: Ernest Churchill and Harry Mews.

Memorial.

There is a tremendous view from the top of the Cross of Sacrifice.

Cement House Cemetery, Langemarck

The cemetery is located 1 km south-west of the village. It was used by fighting units in 1917-1918 and greatly enlarged after the war by the concentration of 2,700 burials from the surrounding area. Cement House was closed for burials in 1925 when it contained 2,938 Commonwealth graves, including 21 Newfoundlanders (10 are unidentified). It was reopened in 1930s for burial of remains found and is open to this day. The cemetery now contains more than 3,500 graves.

Four of the Newfoundland burials (all killed October 14th, 1918), were originally buried in Winkel-St. Eloi Churchyard. They were brought to Cement House in the 1950s. The other 17 Newfoundland graves, all killed in October 1917, were concentrated here prior to 1924.

Duhallow A.D.S. Cemetery, Ypres

The cemetery is located in the northern suburbs of Ypres (Ieper), about 2 km north of the Grote Markt, on the road to Boesinghe. It was opened in July 1917 and used by Casualty Clearing Stations in October-November 1918. After the war 633 remains were brought into the cemetery from the surrounding battlefields. It now contains the graves of 1,544 Commonwealth soldiers including 12 from Newfoundland (Plot IV).

The Newfoundlanders buried here all died of wounds received in action near Keiberg Ridge. Amongst the burials is Second Lieutenant Albert Taylor, MC & Bar, DCM, of Bonavista Bay. Taylor was one of Newfoundland's most decorated soldiers. He had worked his way up the ranks, winning the Distinguished Conduct Medal, a Military Cross at Langemarck in 1917 and a Bar to his MC at Keiberg Ridge. He was mortally wounded October 14th, 1918, and died 3 days later, aged 24. Albert Taylor is buried in IV.G.18.

Dadizeele New British Cemetery

Dadizeele (now Dadizele) is a village 14 km east of Ypres. The cemetery is located on the west side of the village, beside the civilan cemetery. This area was largely behind the lines for the war but saw some action in 1914 and heavy fighting in September-October 1918.

The burials reflect this history, and the majority of the graves belong to soldiers killed in 1918.

The cemetery was made after the war from the concentration of smaller sites and isolated graves from the surrounding battlefields. It now contains 1,029 Commonwealth burials, including 19 Newfoundlanders (all are identified).

The Newfoundland graves reflect two actions; those killed in action on the Keiberg Ridge, October14th, 1918 and a handful killed October 5th, 1918.

In 1914 many British cavalry troopers, captured in the First Battle of Ypres, October 19th-November 22nd, 1914, were marched through Dadizele on their way to Germany. One Trooper of the 2nd Dragoon Guards was offered water by a Belgian boy. The Germans shot both of them. They were buried together in Plot VI, Row D, Grave 21. In 1928 Belgian authorities exhumed the boy's remains (The paperwork states the boy to be Achille Verholle of Moorslede) and removed him to Houthhulst Forest Belgian Military Cemetery, where he was buried as an unknown soldier. In the 1990s efforts were made to put the correct headstone over the boy's grave.

Vichte Military Cemetery

Vichte is a village 8 km east of Courtrai (Kortrijk). The cemetery is located on the west side of the village. It was the scene of heavy fighting by the Royal Newfoundland Regiment and the 9th (Scottish) Division on October 20th-22nd, 1918. The cemetery was made after the battle and was enlarged by the concentration of 138 graves from the surrounding battlefields. It now contains 236 Commonwealth burials including 11 from Newfoundland (3 are unidentified).

The Newfoundlanders are buried in Plot I and are original burials. Of the identified graves 4 were killed in the capture of the Vichte Railway Station on October 20th, 1918 and the others were killed by shelling on October 25th, 1918.

Ingoyghem Military Cemetery, Ingooigem

The village of Ingoyghem (now Ingooigem) is 12 km east of Courtrai (Kortrijk) and 3 km south of Vichte. The cemetery is east of the village and was made after the capture of the village on October 25th, 1918. It now contains 84 Commonwealth graves of which 30 are unidentified. Three graves belong to soldiers of the Royal Newfoundland Regiment. Private Isaac Penny of Brooklyn, Bonvista Bay was killed in action October 26th, 1918, one of the last Newfoundlanders to die in the war. He was 23 years old and the only son of Charles Penny. Private Penny is buried in Row A, Grave 5.

There are Newfoundlanders buried in a number of other cemeteries in the Ypres Salient, principally those who died in the battles fought in 1917. The majority can be found in the following cemeteries: Bard Cottage, Canada Farm, Artillery Wood, Dozinghem Military, Haringhe (Bandighem) Military, Mendinghem Military, Poelcapelle British, and Nine Elms British.

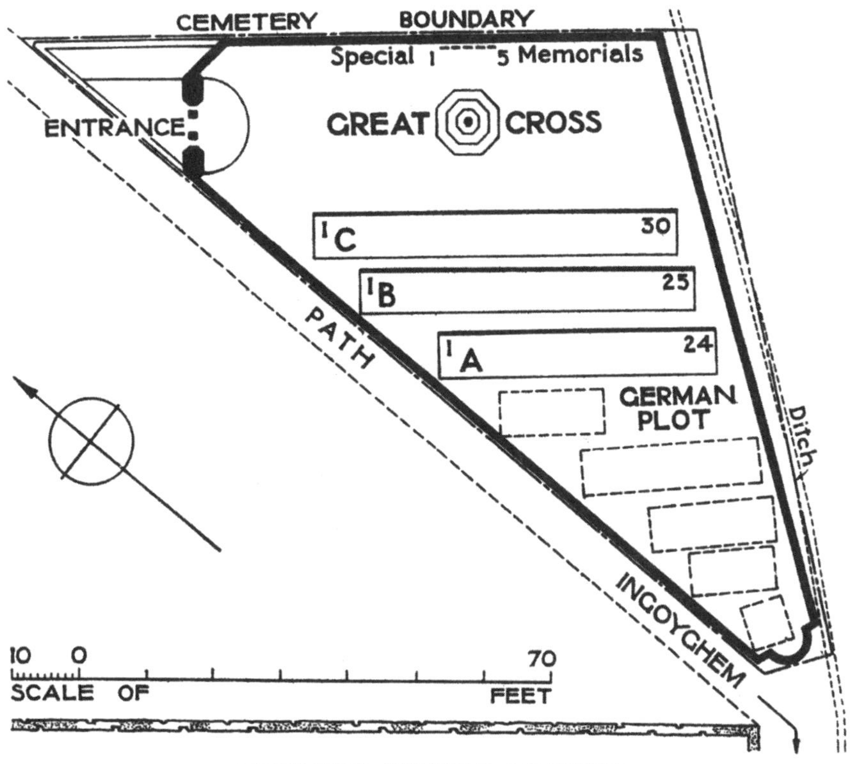

INGOYGHEM MILITARY CEMETERY.

Hospital Areas

Many soldiers wounded in battle were evacuated to Hospital Centres behind the lines or further afield to General Hospitals along the French coast. Those Newfoundlanders who succumbed to their wounds or died of sickness are buried in the following cemeteries.

Duisans British Cemetery, Etrun

The cemetery is located 1 km north of the village, which is 8 km west of Arras on the N39. The cemetery was made by Casualty Clearing Stations and the burials reflect the great offensives of 1917 and 1918. It contains the graves of 3,211 Commonwealth soldiers including 12 from Newfoundland.

Most of the Newfoundlanders buried here died of wounds received at Monchy, April 14th, 1917.

The entrance feature of the cemetery is pock-marked with bullet holes from May 1940 when French Colonial troops tried to hold up the advancing Nazis.

Etaples Military Cemetery

Etaples was the major depot base for the British Army on the Western Front and was the location of the infamous Bull Ring and the British Mutiny of 1917. Etaples Military Cemetery is located on the coastal road (D940) between Boulogne and Le Touquet. It is 3 km north of Le Touquet. It was used throughout the war for the burials of soldiers who died of wounds or of sickness. It contains the graves of 10,729 Commonwealth soldiers from every corner of the world. Scattered amongst the burials are the graves of 18 Newfoundlanders.

Those buried here reflect every battle in 1916-1917 in which the Newfound Regiment fought. Second Lieutenant Clifford Rendell died July 22nd, 1916 of wounds received at Beaumont-Hamel (I.A.38). He was 21 years old. His brother, Captain Herbert Rendell, MC, was killed September 29th, 1918 and is buried in Dadizele British Cemetery (VI.F.16.). He was 29. They were the sons of Herbert and Lizzie Rendell of St, John's.

Buried in Plot XXXI, Row B, Grave 18 is Private Stephen Janes of Pilley's Island. He died of wounds, December 6th, 1917, received in the Battle of Cambrai. He was 25. His 29 year old brother, George

Robert Janes was killed at Beaumont-Hamel, July 1st, 1916. He is commemorated by name only on the Beaumont-Hamel Memorial.

Terlincthun British Cemetery, Wimille

Wimille is a hamlet 4 km north of Boulogne. The cemetery is located in a hollow south of the hamlet. From the cemetery there is a view of the English Channel and Napoleon's Column. The coastal region is lined with Second World War German bunkers.

The cemetery was opened in the summer of 1918 when the cemeteries at Boulogne and Wimereux were full. It was used by hospitals in the area into 1919. It contained 3,011 burials in 1922 but years later it was reopened for burials and it still receives the remains found in the fields and villages of France. The current statistics for the cemetery list 4,438 graves, including 10 Newfoundlanders.

St. Sever Communal Cemetery and Extension, Rouen

Rouen is the capital of Normandy. It is 150 km south-west of Arras.

It was a major Headquarters, supply, transport and medical centre for the British Army throughout the war. The Hospitals buried their dead in the plots adjacent to the civilian cemetery at St. Sever, south of the Seine River. Over the years the British Cemetery grew enormously to finally hold 11,376 graves, making it the largest Commonwealth cemetery in France. The burials are comprised of every Nationality in the Empire and beyond. There are British, Australian, New Zealanders, Canadians, South Africans, British West Indians, Indians, Egyptians, Chinese, Italians, one Portugese and 16 Newfoundlanders buried in St. Sever Communal Cemetery or its Extension. There are also a number of Commonwealth Second World War graves in the cemetery. The First Canadian Army liberated Rouen in 1944. Joan of Arc was burned in Rouen in earlier times.

One of the Newfoundlanders buried in the Communal Cemetery, Officers B.19.28., is Second Lieutenant Samuel Ebsary, age 37, who died of wounds October 15th, 1916, received at Gueudecourt. He was one of the oldest Newfoundlanders to die in the war. His much younger brother, Frederick, died September 23rd, 1915, in hospital in Cairo, Egypt. He is buried in the Cairo War Memorial Cemetery, D.112.

Lieutenant-Colonel Tom Nangle.

Rudolph Cochius. (Cochius)

The cabin in Beaumont-Hamel Park, circa 1924. (Cochius)

"Holy Ground"

Newfoundland Memorial Park, Beaumont-Hamel

Today along the old Western Front very little evidence remains of the ferocious and brutal battles that took place in 1914-1918. A handful of bunkers and shell holes, now grassed over, mark the locales where thousands of men lost their lives. The memorials that remain, such as the casements of Verdun or the Canadian monument at Vimy, are overgrown; and one would require a clear understanding of the battle itself to get the real sense of what a battlefield was like in the First World War. It is only at Beaumont-Hamel that the plight of the Great War soldier is apparent.

The idea for such a memorial stems from one man, Reverend Tom Nangle. Nangle was the Catholic Chaplain in the Newfoundland Regiment from November 1916 until the end of the war. He was an impressive man, who went into the line with the men, faced their dangers and shared their hardships. The Padre found a special place in the hearts of the Newfoundlanders and was immensely popular with all, regardless of denomination. His sincere concern raised morale, and within a short time Father Nangle became the heart and soul of the Regiment. It was said that he "certainly has the knack of bringing to the down-hearted the necessary good cheer, which he never seems to be wanting himself."

Thomas Mathew Mary Nangle was born in St. John's in 1888. His parents died young and Tom was raised in an orphanage. He was educated in a strict Catholic school, St. Bonaventure's College, entered the Seminary and was ordained as a Priest in June 1913. When war was declared the young Nangle tried to join the First Contingent as a soldier, but this was stopped by the Church. Perhaps as an act of compensation, Tom Nangle was chosen to be a Newfoundland Catholic Chaplain overseas. He reached the Field in November 1916, just after Gueudecourt, and served with the Regiment until the end of the war. He was constantly with the men and even organized an ice hockey match on an ice-cold winter's day at the village of Coisy. It was Nangle's squad versus Major Tait's, the Adjutant's six. Sadly he was also there to bury the dead, many of them being his friends and his peers.

The war affected the young Priest dramatically. The sacrifices of his fellow Newfoundlanders cut him deeply, so much so that preserving the

Memory of "Ours", as he referred to them, became his Life's mission. It was in 1919 as Lieutenant-Colonel Tom Nangle, Newfoundland's Representative with Directorate of Graves and Enquiries and the Imperial War Graves Commission, that this mission took form.

His first task was to find and mark the graves of as many Newfoundlanders he could find on the old battlefields. In 1919-1920 this was a daunting and depressing job. With great persistence Father Tom located and photographed every grave he could find, sending copies to the families in Newfoundland. Sadly the graves of many of those killed or missing were never found, "I'm afraid the task is hopeless and that very few identifications will be made," he wrote in 1919.

His second task was to commemorate the actions of the Newfoundland Regiment in the Great War. To do this he developed the idea of "The Trail of the Caribou". He wanted to mark the five most significant battlefields with a memorial unique to Newfoundland, so that these places would forever be a piece of Newfoundland. In 1919 he commissioned the British sculptor, Basil Gotto (1866-1954) to carve a massive caribou, modeled on the photo known as "The Monarch of the Topsails" (pronounced Topsills). "The Monarch" was a powerful stag caribou, with his head held high, defiantly sounding his battle-cry. Gotto was to produce the sculpture and six bronze castings would be made, one for each of the five battlefields and the sixth for Bowring Park in St. John's. (He entertained 16 potential designs for the memorials, but appeared to have already determined what he wanted.) Each caribou would rest on a crag of granite.

He stated that "The Battle Exploit Memorials are being erected by the other Dominions to show Europe and the World what the Dominions have done. They are monuments to our Glorious Dead and to our just as glorious survivors. They are monuments to the mothers that bore such brave sons and the land that bred them."

The battlefields he selected were: Beaumont-Hamel, Gueudecourt, Masnieres, Monchy (in the town or on Infantry Hill) and the Keiberg Ridge (or near Courtrai). There were many memorials being erected in the 1920s and there was often a competition between various groups. The French government was getting so many applications that the sites had to be limited. In the end Nangle got approval for his choices and obtained the locations of preference. The idea for all the Memorial Parks was the same. The bronze Caribou would be placed on a granite

Beaumont-Hamel, circa 1922. (Cochius)

Beaumont-Hamel, circa 1922.
(Cochius)

Artificial mound being prepared, circa 1923. (Cochius)

Basil Gotto with his sculpture, "The Monarch of the top-sails."

rock crag facing the direction the Newfoundlanders met the enemy.

To raise money for the Memorials Father Nangle made an appeal to all the People of Newfoundland. He visited every town and tiny, isolated Outport, by every means available: train, car or by foot. He made a point of visiting the families of the Fallen and became a source of inspiration in many communities. Tirelessly he pursued his mission to create a special Memorial at Beaumont-Hamel.

In June 1919 he made his proposal for the Memorial Park to Sir William Coaker, a prominent Newfoundland politician. Coaker immediately agreed with Nangle and obtained $10,000 to buy the land. Over the next three years Father Tom dealt with 250 odd landowners, residing from Dunkirk to Morocco, before the land became Newfoundland's.

In the 1920s there was a severe shortage of qualified labour in France and Nangle's early efforts at constructing the sites (known as Battle Exploit Memorials), fell dismally behind schedule. His fortunes changed when he located and employed the Dutch landscape architect, Rudolph H.K. Cochius. Originally from Arnhem, Cochius had been working in Newfoundland since 1911 and had designed, amongst other things, Bowring Park in St. John's. He was a man of exceptional talent, who also had a piece of his heart on the Island where three of his five children were born. In 1922 Cochius uprooted his family, moved to Albert and set to work on "The Trail of the Caribou". Both men shared deep feelings for their task and between Tom Nangle's personal passion and the skill of Rudolph Cochius, Beaumont-Hamel was born.

In 1922 Cochius, now residing in a war-ravaged Albert, had opened the Newfoundland War Memorials office at 14 rue Hurtu. There in the living room he and Tom Nangle worked put the projects together. He built a Newfoundland-style log cabin in the Park to accommodate Pilgrims, dug out the old trenches, surrounded the entire 40 acres with a fence and dug the foundation for Gotto's monument. Massive granite slabs were purchased in the Ardennes and transported to the sites. He brought in 35,000 trees from Scotland, Holland and Newfoundland. Finally in 1922 the first Caribou at Gueudecourt was in place. Masnieres was finished shortly after. Cochius also worked on the sites of the 51st Highland Division Memorial (unveiled September 28th, 1924) and the 29th Division Memorial located within the Park (on land given by Newfoundland). Cochius himself unveiled a new member of his own family when a son, Rudolph, was born in Albert in 1923. But his work

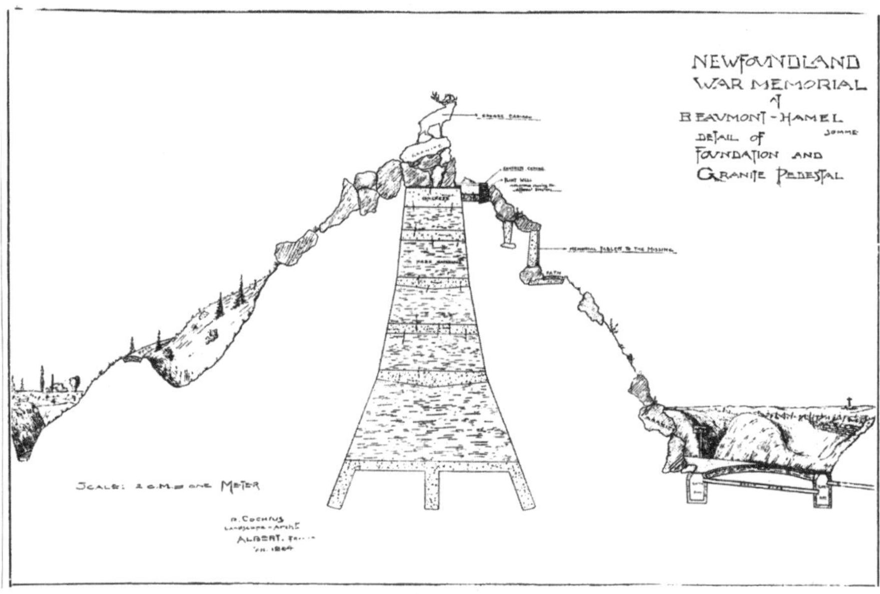

Rudolph Cochius' sketches.

at Beaumont-Hamel was truly his greatest task.

Of Beaumont-Hamel Rudoph Cochius wrote "a fitting memorial to those whom it commemorates, cannot but materialize in an achievement of which all Newfoundlanders will take pride... it will be the impressiveness of the whole place that will make Newfoundland Park at Beaumont-Hamel a place of Pilgrimage, not only for Newfoundlanders and Anglo-Saxons, but for the French and others as well, as it is the only place along the whole front where part of the battlefield is being preserved". He had been in Newfoundland on July 1st and knew of the Battle's terrible impact on the people. Rudolph Cochius knew the importance of Beaumont-Hamel and he would not disappoint.

In early 1925 the Park was ready. The Caribou stood defiantly atop his granite cliff, surrounded by native trees. Cochius had indeed created a piece of Newfoundland in the heart of war-torn France. At the base of the Caribou three bronze panels were erected commemorating the "Missing" of Newfoundland. The official Unveiling was scheduled for June 7th, 1925.

The experience was also emotional for Rudolph Cochius. "Standing on the high plateau overlooking the British, and German trenches, lower down, my mind reverted to those terrible days in St. John's following that never to be forgotten 1st of July and again I saw that tense and silent crowd patiently, yet impatiently, waiting in front of the Post Office and the bulletins elsewhere on Water Street, in anxious apprehension, scanning each successive telegram that appeared - some to receive the news they feared most, some to await with stimulated hope for some later bulletin. And then I saw again, actually before me, these trenches, no-man's-land, strewn thick with barbed wire, countless shell holes and more sinister still, broken rifles, torn equipment, steel helmets, so many with that tiny hole that indicated only too well that some enemy bullet had found its mark."

The ceremonies at the Caribou Memorial were preceded by the unveiling of the 29th Division Memorial. The actual unveiling of the Newfoundland Memorial fell to Field Marshal Earl Haig, who had commanded the British Army from 1915-1919. He was accompanied by a number of dignitaries from France, Britain and Newfoundland and escorted by a French and British Guard of Honour and a Veteran's Guard.

The Field Marshal delivered his address. "Officers and men, the rep-

Cochius family at their home and "Newfoundland War Memorials' office in Albert, 1922. (Cochius)

Tom Nangle toasts the dignitaries, including F.M. Earl Haig, June 1925 (Cochius)

Beaumont-Hamel, circa 1925.

Field Marshal Earl Haig and Lt. Col. Thomas Nangle at the opening of Beaumont-Hamel Park, June 7th, 1925.

The Opening of Beaumont-Hamel Park, June 7th, 1925.

Field Marshal Earl Haig and Lt. Col. Thomas Nangle at the opening of Beaumont-Hamel Park, June 7th, 1925. (PANF)

resentatives today of that Newfoundland Battalion which in the days of the Great War gave such gallant service to Newfoundland and the Empire: - We are here on a solemn occasion, and at a spot which is for all of us is full of memories. Yet, solemn though it be, it is not an occasion for sorrow; for we are here to unveil a memorial which will remind generations still unborn of the loyalty and courage of Newfoundland men, and of the unity and strength of the mighty Empire which is our pride and inheritance.

"...These slopes where fell so many of your best and bravest, are sacred to their memory. Here your comrades died in the hope of that victory which they would never see. Today that victory is achieved, you set up in the place where they died a monument to their faith and their courage. This memorial, then, is evidence of the spirit of your men; a spirit which ill fortune could not quench...

"...You send a message to the spirits of those Newfoundlanders whose bodies lie buried far from their own land, that the place of their final resting is nor forgotten... This memorial to your dead, set up in a foreign but friendly land will be a challenge to all who see it, generation after generation, reminding them of the solidarity of the British peoples of the Empire in whatsoever part of the world they have made their homes, are ready and willing to make for the security of the Empire and for the peace of the world; and setting an example to future generations of our own race of what their fathers did and what they may one day be called upon to do."

After a short speech by French General Fayolle, the Vicar-General of Amiens performed the Dedication, and then Earl Haig pulled the silken cord which caused the Union Jack and the Tricolour to fall from the Caribou. It was followed by a two minute silence and concluded with the Last Post being sounded by buglers of the Royal Scots.

Field Marshal Haig and General Fayolle laid the first wreaths at the base of the Memorial followed by hundreds of other floral tributes. Amonst the wreaths laid was one placed by Cochius' daughters on behalf of the children of Newfoundland.

Today much of the original Park is gone. The broken rifles, tin helmets and barbed wire have disappeared. The sandbags have rotted away and the trenches subsided. The log house, where Haig was received after the ceremony, burned down and was replaced by the current Superintendent's house in 1961. But it is still an extraspecial place and

Tom Nangle and Rudolph Cochius, pipes in hand, at Beaumont-Hamel Park circa 1923. (Cochius)

as Tom Nangle stated in 1926 "... if Beaumont-Hamel is preserved with reasonable attention it will remain not only a great tribute to the force of Newfoundland, but also will go down to posterity as the greatest historical memorial of what the Great War actually meant." As usual he got it right, Beaumont-Hamel continues to be "Holy ground".

Postscript

In 1921, at the height of his effort to create "The Trail of the Caribou" Tom Nangle left the Priesthood (which was a difficult thing to do in a very religious Newfoundland). His terrible experiences of war and watching the sacrifice and suffering of innocent men caused him to lose his Faith. He continued with the IWGC until after the Unveiling of Beaumont-Hamel in 1925. With his mission completed Nangle left for Rhodesia where he farmed, mined and became a Member of Parliament. In 1929 he married a Rhodesian, Thelma Watkinson, and later they had four children. He returned to Beaumont-Hamel only once for the 50th Anniversary of the Battle in 1966. He never did return to Newfoundland. Tom Nangle died in January 1972 and is buried in Que-Que, Rhodesia. Beaumont-Hamel remained to him the most important thing he ever did.

Rudolph Cochius returned to Newfoundland to work until the mid 1930s when he moved to Montreal. He returned to Beaumont-Hamel only once with his eldest daughter in 1936. In 1943 he was commissioned to landscape the Stations of the Cross on Mount Royal. In March of that year, while at work on his design, he suffered a heart attack and died. Rudolph Cochius is buried in Montreal Memorial Park, Outremont. He was 65 years old. His son, Rudolph, born in Albert during the construction of Newfoundland Park, enlisted with the Canadian Army in Montreal. He landed on Juno Beach with the Cameron Highlanders of Ottawa on June 6th, 1944. Private Cochius was killed in action the next day. He is buried in Beny-sur-Mer Canadian War Cemetery, Normandy, Plot IV, Row A, Grave 1. Rudolph Albert Cochius was 20 years old.

For Further Reference

There have been more books written on the Battle of the Somme than on all other battles of the First World War combined, so there is no shortage of material, fiction, non-fiction, memoirs or guides. Other battles such as Arras, 1917 or Cambrai, 1917 are not as well recorded.

I have listed below a few of the best on the battlefields and on the Newfoundland Regiment itself. Although this guide deals solely with the five battles commemorated by the Government of Newfoundland, there is a great deal to see on the Western Front. Cemeteries and Memorials commemorate the sacrifices of so many nations; such as Britain, France, India, South Africa, Canada, New Zealand and Australia. Visiting these "sacred places" is a rewarding experience.

Battlefield Guides

Before Endeavours Fade, by Rose E, Coombs. Battle of Britain, 1976.

Australian Battlefields of the Western Front, by John Laffin. Kangaroo Press, 1992.

The Somme Battlefields, by M. Middlebrook. Viking Press, 1981.

Pilgrimage, by W.D. Parsons. Creative Publishing, 1994.

For King & Empire; Vols. 1-9, by N.M. Christie. CEF Books, 1996-2003.

The Royal Newfoundland Regiment

The First Day on the Somme, by M.Middlebrook. Alen Lane, 1971.

The Fighting Newfoundlander, G.W.L. Nicholson. Government of Newfoundland, 1964.

The Danger Tree, by D. MacFarlane. MacFarlane, Walter & Ross, 1991.

Memoir of a Blue Puttee, by A.J. Stacey. DRC Publishers, 2002.

Letters of Mayo Lind, by Francis T. Lind. Creative Publishing, 2001.

Trail of the Caribou, by R.H. Tait, MC. Newfoundland Pub., 1933.

Lieutenant Owen William Steele of the Newfoundland Regiment, ed. by D.R. Facey-Crowther. McGill-Queen's University Press, 2002.